COMMUNITY PARTICIPATION AND SUSTAINABLE FOREST DEVELOPMENT

About the Author

Dr. A.K. Bhattacharya is all India topper of 1983 batch of Indian Forest Service. He is Doctorate in Environmental Science (Ecology). Presently he is serving M. P. Forest Department as Deputy Conservator of Forests at Bhopal. He possesses research and practical experience of seventeen years in the fields of Environmental Science and Forestry. He has contributed large number of research papers and articles in the above fields. The present book is an outcome of the project report submitted by him in the University of Tasmania, Australia as a part of the six months course on Sustainable Forestry Development.

COMMUNITY PARTICIPATION AND SUSTAINABLE FOREST DEVELOPMENT
Global Perspective

AJOY KUMAR BHATTACHARYA
Deputy Conservator of Forests
Bhopal (M.P.)

CONCEPT PUBLISHING COMPANY, NEW DELHI-110059

ISBN 81-7022-890-5

First Published 2001

Published and Printed by
Ashok Kumar Mittal
Concept Publishing Company
A/15-16, Commercial Block, Mohan Garden
New Delhi-110059 (India)
Phones: 5648039, 5649024
Fax: 091–(11)–5648053
Email: publishing@conceptpub.com

Preamble

'We must have a true participation of all of the society in the decision making and more particularly in the allocation of resources. And why so? Because all of us are perfectly aware that there will never be sufficient resources for everything that we wish, but if the population participates in decision making it will benefit those who need the most and it will express their thought about the allocation of resources and it will give us the certainty that which is being done is the legitimate aspiration of the people.'

(World Commission on Environment and Development)

There is a crucial need for both developed and developing countries to analyse the rules of global crisis of forest management as it manifests itself and affects the whole world, and specifically for people in third world to advocate a different form of society, a different type of development.

It is important to see the world forest management problems not only from the level of the community, or even the nation, but as an integral component of a global system of industrialisation which shapes the way and the rate in which forest resources are exploited and used and which therefore determines not only how environments are more different, recreated or disrupted, but also how people's very lives are affected.

Eliciting authentic community participation in forest management is difficult and time-consuming in developed countries and even more so in developing nations. But evidence from previous experience has conformed one of the principle lessons from resource management projects: that the sustainability of forest resource depends strongly on the effective participation of local people. This means more than participation as beneficiaries or as paid employees. Rather, it means participation in decision making, in problem identification, in project design and implementation, and in project monitoring and evaluation. This approach views local development as a process rather than a product with project personnel performing a facilitating role. Establishment of a process of local participation has proved to be a more effective method of sustaining forest resources than approaches that attempt to deliver economic benefits without involving local people or building commitment to the outcome of the forest resource management.

Contents

List of Figures

Executive Summary

The book embodies information on the relevant sections and excerpts pertaining to community participation in forest management, from the original forest acts, policies and other documents of different countries and international organisations. An attempt has been made to review and examine these forest acts, policies and other forestry linked documents and recommendations of forestry linked international organisations, including United Nations Food and Agricultural Organisation, other organisations of United Nations, World Bank and various countries. The recommendation of the Rio Earth Summit and Agenda 21 have also been examined.

The relevant sections and paras of the policies and acts have been quoted and reproduced to understand the approach and change in trends in the world view on the community participation in Sustainable Forest Management. An overall view of the analysis of the acts and laws has been presented.

In both developed and developing countries the forest policies and acts indicate a change in varying degrees in the trend of forest management from top-bottom approach to bottom-top approach. Community participation has been globally accepted as a concept and essential tool for the sustainability of forest resource.

The forest policies and acts tend to reflect the changed global view and most of them have been revised to include community participation as an essential component of sustainable forest management.

In developing countries the forest policies and acts lay an emphasis on the forest communities interface in terms of benefits and sharing of products and profits and there is a concern about the role of communities in the protection of forests, whereas in developed countries the community participation has been considered necessary for exchange of information, education and training and the forest policies reflect a concern about the recreation of the communities through forestry, like ecotourism.

The recommendations of the Rio Earth Summit and Agenda 21 on Sustainable Forest Management centre around community participation and the necessity for community participation for Sustainable Forest Management has been clearly spelt out in various chapters. The need for involving communities at various levels including decision making, sharing of benefits, positive role of non-governmental organisations have been categorically enunciated.

In Australia the community participation has gained a momentum as all policies and acts include community participation as a component of forestry related programmes. The Tasmanian Forest Departments have elaborate systems for public participation through media and seminars for inviting public opinions on government programmes. The public participation mechanism is being used as a tool for generating an effective information network system. Community involvement in decision making and sharing of benefits and incentives for communities are the issues which need to be addressed more explicitly in both policies and actual implementation. The policies lay adequate emphasis on the recreational values of the forest resource for communities.

The concept of community participation for forest protection has attracted much attention in India during the late 1980s. The 1988 Forest Policy has been the milestone for the recent change in approach and is basically a people oriented forest policy. The policy has clear provisions for direct community participation in decision making, sharing of usufructs and the policy intends to empower the communities to take decisions to manage the forest for their sustainability.

Although the detailed forest policies and acts of other countries have not been examined critically and some of the reviewed policies and acts are not the latest editions, nevertheless a distinct indication emerges from ali the available documents of a shifting over from production forestry to people oriented forestry.

Although community participation has been widely accepted as an essential key element and prerequisite for sustainable forest management, nevertheless no pragmatic and effective device for active community involvement has so far been evolved. It thus becomes imperative that specific workable models for community participation are required to be evolved to institutionalise the co-operative relationship between forests and the local people.

The World Bank report on various government programmes on community involvement in sustainable forest management and Community Aid Abroad report on NGOs' programmes for community participation in forestry linked activities both indicate that present models with respect to sustainable forest management have not been effective (World Bank 1995, Blackburn 1993).

The individual experiences of various countries and organisations on community involvement have not been coordinated and integrated so as to arrive at any concrete module based on all the positive and best features of the existing models of community participation. Since in most of the developing countries the community participation is at initial taking off stage, it is essential to critically evaluate the mechanisms of community participation and examine their strengths and weaknesses so as to institutionalise the process.

There is substantial scope for further research work to analyse the forest policies and acts for necessary revisions to match the requirements of the people, so as to institutionalise the concept of community involvement as a system. The strengths and weaknesses of policies and acts may further be critically analysed and the possibility of a 'holistic integrated ecosystem approach' may be investigated.

1

Prologue

'Forestry for the people' was the theme for the 8th world Forestry Congress held in 1978 in Djakarta, Indonesia. Since then the experience and knowledge gained over the two decades have led to the global acceptance of community as the most effective and indispensable path towards the sustainable development.

The Rio Summit of 1992, which happened to be the turning point in the world environmental history, paved another milestone in the way of sustainability and further strengthened the concept of community participation for the Sustainable Forest Management.

Almost all the international organisations including IUCN (World Resources Institute 1992, FAO 1985, 1991, 1996, World Bank 1992), have recognised the effectiveness of the community involvement technique as a management tool for the Sustainable Forest Management and at the same time have emphasised upon the necessity of intensive research works for the analyses of the existing knowledge on community participation and exploring different viable practical models for using community involvement as an effective tool and its institutionalisation for Sustainable Forest Management.

At national levels the experiences of the developing countries (Ahlback 1995, Bundyard 1989, Mgeni 1992, Schwartz 1989, Srisarin 1994) indicate that community involvement has been adopted as a future strategy for Sustainable Forest Management and so far marginal success has been achieved and, therefore, more efforts are required to institutionalise community participation as a system.

In the light of the phenomenal increase in the population of human and livestock and the consequential intense biotic pressure on the forests of the developing countries, community participation mechanism has been recognised as an essential element in strategies for Sustainable Forest Management, since the forests can be protected only with the active collaboration the of local communities.

The necessity for the community involvement as an effective tool for the long term sustainable management of the protected areas has also been proved beyond doubt (Bahuguna, Luthra & Rathore 1994, Lay 1996, Sadler 1990, Wells & Brandon 1995, Wight 1993). Furthermore, most of the case studies and reports (Arnold 1991, Chaplin 1989, Gadgil 1992, Rastogi 1995, Sharma 1995, Blackburn 1993) indicate that the success of the community participation in sustainable forest management requires tremendous research works particularly the understanding of the socio-economic and technical issues in order to evolve some specific models which can match the requirements of the linkages between the forests and the local communities.

In order to institutionalise the concept of community participation for sustainable forest management it is essential to review the forest policies and bring about necessary changes, reforms and modifications in the legislative, administrative and legal changes in the laws and rules and regulations communicating the requirements and vision of the people.

Policies are designed to benefit people: but whom? There may be conflicts of interest between the population as a whole and those living in or near forests or depending on forests and forest products for their living, especially woodland owners and all who work in the forest or wood processing industries. It is in the poorest countries where the majority of people live in rural areas and depend entirely on forest produce for many necessities of life, including wood fuel to cook their food. The interests of these people should be paramount although they usually have little political influence (Hummel 1984).

It may also not always be easy to reconcile the achievement of immediate benefits with maintaining and if possible improving the long term production potential of forests. The individual is generally mainly concerned with the benefits that may accrue during his life time, the politician with what happens before the next election.

Forest policies and other policies must be consistent with each other and where there are conflicts of interest, these must be resolved. Forest policy is an important component of land use policy, in the absence of which it is difficult to develop a sensible forest policy. There are also links with other policies: those concerned with agriculture, the environment, industry, trade, employment, regional development, to name some of the more important. What is however, crucial is that forest policy must be developed as a coherent whole instead of as a series of appendages to these other policies. It is only when forest policy is developed as a sector policy in its own right that the various aspects of forest policy can be properly co-ordinated. The co-ordination of policies is greatly facilitated within the framework of *regional* policies because every region has some specific characteristics and problems.

Finally, forest policy formation is a continuing process. Policy must be adjusted in the light of changing physical and economic circumstances and changing demands by the various sectors of society. It is, however, a great advantage if forest policy is not made the subject of party politics. Forest policy must be progressive, but frequent changes of direction are bound to harm any long term enterprise such as forestry.

2

Sustainable Forest Management and Sustainable Development

Over the past two decades, the international forestry community has come to recognise the linkages between meeting the needs of people for natural resources and conserving or protecting the natural environment. This "linkage" has been recognised in the phrase of Sustainable Development. A convergence of the diverse thinking on this linkage was captured by the World Commission on Environment and Development's 1987 report "Our Common Future". The report provided a commonly accepted (although very general) definition for sustainable development that was reaffirmed at the Earth Summit in 1992 in Brazil:

Sustainable Development is "development that meets the needs of the present without compromising the ability of future generations to meet their own needs."

Different groups have developed variations of this definition to suit their own perceived needs, none of which have generated any consensus.

2.1 Principles of Sustainable Activity

The principles of sustainable development attribute the following characteristics:

* adaptable to change;
* integration of ecological, cultural, and ecosystem systems;

* does not foreclose options to future generations;
* current resource or social conditions may not be maintainable;
* based on public support and local solutions;
* the costs and benefits of forest management are shared by all;
* using sustainable development to find common ground;
* site, ecosystem, regional, national, or global; and
* threshold values for a number of identified elements.

Sustainability is also defined as a set of characteristics (criteria and indicators). Indicators measured over time are used to indicate trends in those characteristics (WCED 1990).

Whilst development had traditionally been painted as the enemy of conservation, it has since been found that this need not be the case. A development activity is sustainable if use remains within natural yields and waste assimilation abilities of the natural environment (Perch and Turner 1990). Development is thus only constrained by the ability of technology and social organisation to manage its sustainability (WCED 1990).

"The sustainable development discussion has demonstrated that development is dependent on the conservation of the environment, and that conservation is dependent on development. This link or integration of conservation and development were first recognised by the World Conservation Strategy in 1980 (Gubbay 1995). The resources and biodiversity which reside in ecosystems are necessary for agricultural and industrial production are the foundations of development. Governments now recognise that conservation of the environment in protected area systems is essential for sustainable economic development in a variety of ways (McNeely 1995). Conservation is dependent on development to improve both technology and human capacity to manage sustainable resource use. This is particularly true in areas with low developmental levels because poverty is frequently a major cause of environmental degradation" (Grun 1996).

The world's top political leadership now recognises that natural resource management must be an integral part of sustainable development. Sustainable forest management is the forestry sector's part of sustainable development.

2.2 Sustainable Forest Management provides

* a better umbrella concept for diverse views on forest management than anything now used;
* a vehicle for developing consensus;
* help to focus efforts in ecosystem management;
* a functional and intersectoral integrating concept; and
* complements existing Forest Service initiatives and programmes activities.

2.3 Sustainable Development, Sustainable Forest Management, and Ecosystem Management

There is a need to differentiate among sustainable development, sustainable forest management, and ecosystem management. The distinctions among them are blurred to many people. In the economic development literature, sustainable forest management is considered to be a subset of sustainable development. Cross sectoral issues relevant to sustainable development policy therefore might not be addressed in development of sustainable forest management policy. A strategy for sustainable development, therefore, must harmonise policies across sectors. It follows that sustainable forest management policies should also consider other sector policies but may not be able to incorporate them (for example, sustainable forest management policy may have to presume eventual policies on population growth). In the end, this will have to be reconciled.

Ecosystem management, as applied by the Forest Service, means the integration of ecological, economic, and social factors on public lands to best meet current and future needs of people and the environment. Ecosystem management is, therefore, the means of achieving the goal of sustainable forest management and in turn, sustainable development.

2.4 Community Participation and Sustainable Development

Once the concept of sustainable development had been discovered and internationally introduced by the World Conservation Strategy (WCS) and World Commission on the Environment and Development (WCED), the next step was to find a way of achieving it. In 1989, on the recommendation of the WCED the United Nations passed a resolution which established the United Nations Conference on the Environment and Development (UNCED). In Rio de Janeiro in June 1992, 178 countries signed five major agreements including Agenda 21, the Rio declaration on sustainable development and the Convention on Biological Diversity (CBD). Agenda 21 and the Global Biodiversity Strategy (GBS) 1992, which is complementary to the CBD, propose detailed strategies for achieving sustainable development and for conserving biological diversity respectively (UNCED, WRI, IUCN, UNEP 1992).

Agenda 21 and the GBS served to crystallise ideas that had been explored over the previous two or three decades, including the ICDP, MAB Programme and the IUCN changes. The new approaches which resulted aim to improve resource management by incorporating the social, political and economic and developmental concerns in order to effectively manage the human systems which control resource use and development. More specifically, sustainable management should:

(a) be equitable by considering the needs of local people;
(b) be interdisciplinary to facilitate integration of broader social political and economic factors in resource management;
(c) alleviate poverty and build capacity for sustainable resource management;
(d) involve the public in management, including indigenous people, women, youth, businesses, scientific communities and Non-Governmental Organisations (NGOs); and
(e) be based on decentralised decision making at regional and local levels (MacKinnon *et al.,* 1986, Korten 1986, McNeely 1988, Fiske 1992, Lusigi in Munasinghe and McNeely 1994, Metcalfe in Munasinghe and McNeely 1994, Adede

1992, Wells and Brandon 1992, WRI, IUCN, UNEP 1992, UNCED website, Gubbay 1995 and McNeely 1995).

Increasingly, community participation is recognised as a mechanism for implementing sustainable development by institutionalising the five approaches listed above. Community management, which includes a varying degree of public participation, maximised all sources knowledge and interest in conservation, including local users, those with vested interests and indigenous groups. Community management aims to empower local groups to take an active role in improving conservation and development, which benefits local communities and makes use of all human resources available for conservation. Community participation requires significant support from government agencies, as it represents a turnaround from previously centralised government decision making.

2.5 Elements of Community Participation

The following is a list of the potential elements of a community participation in resource management (Grun 1996).

Background Information

* Community surveys, interviews and meetings for discussion to determine community and environmental needs and constraints and assemble all available knowledge.
* Community involvement gathering new environmental and socio-economic information.
* Community organisers or liaison personnel can introduce concepts and discuss possibilities, gather information and make recommendations.

Awareness and Capacity Building

* Conservation education and awareness campaigns: formal and informal.

* Training programs to develop management skills and improved resource techniques.
* Support from media and NGO groups, academics and academic institutions.

Community Participation in Planning and Decision Making

* Consultation through meetings, discussions, surveys.
* Advisory Committees.
* Management Committees: include local people, authorities, user organisations.
* Strengthen users organisations.
* Procedures should be transparent to prevent corruption.
* Community should participate in the formulation of rules, regulations, zones.
* The purpose of regulation should be understood by the community.
* Regulations must be enforceable and enforced.
* Decisions should identify causal link between impacts and behaviour, determine solutions or alternatives and be flexible to adapt to changes.
* Decision making and planning should be interactive and may involve mediation, negotiation or joint problem solving between different interests.
* Regular communication between managers, scientists and community.

Improve Developmental Status of Community to Reduce Pressure on Environmental Resources and to Compensate for Decreased Access to Resources

* Basic Social services: health clinics.
* Alternative sources of income that diversifies local economies.
* Improved resources management through training and research programmes.

Implementation

* Members of the community should be employed to carry out construction, maintenance and monitoring and enforcement in protected area.
* Concessionary services, such as tour guides, accommodation and souvenir stores should be provided and managed by community members.

Monitoring and Evaluation

* Monitoring and evaluation of environmental quality and management effectiveness to determine possible improvements.
* Social impact assessments.

Research

* Biological and physical processes.
* Better resource use techniques.
* Social, economic, political and cultural issues that effect conservation and sustainable management of resources.

Indigenous Culture and Knowledge

* Develop skills and programmes to learn from and conserve indigenous knowledge, practices and environmental management systems.

Supportive Government or Non-government Agencies can provide

* Legislative framework within which community participation is legally formalised and a clear jurisdiction to work within.
* Assist defining management norms and regulation.
* Broad policy framework and institutional support and basic social

services that improve the developmental status of communities near protected areas.

* Provide expert and scientific advice and information.
* Supervise management, provide a national and international perspective on conservation.
* Provide judicial and policing functions.
* Facilitate communication and co-ordination with existing structures: local government, legislation, regional planning.
* Necessary funding.
* Government and Non-government agencies should be oriented towards decentralised decision making and community participation.

Community Management is successful if

* Improved relationships within communities and between communities and agencies are formed that facilitate communication and co-operation to achieve sustainable resource management.
* There is growth in community confidence in their ability to change and improve their actions to implement sustainable resource management.

3

Forest Policies and Community Participation for Sustainable Forest Management

Forests are the most developed and widespread vegetation cover of our planet and everyday almost everyone out of the myriads of the people in the world is, willingly or not, using or consuming some product or service from the forests.

The role of the forests and forest management in our everyday life is thus obvious. Shrinking forests and lack of and/or failure of forestry have become global issues.

Forestry is the management and use for human benefit of the natural resources that occur on or in association with forest lands and other lands managed wholly or in part for similar purposes.

Every nation needs to formulate and implement a forest policy for a definite course or method of action (as by government, institutions, groups or individual) from among alternatives and in the light of given conditions to guide and usually determine future decisions.

The forest policy has to balance in one way or the other the relationship of society with its forest resource. Even in the most simple situation for instance a tribe living in the forest, the link between the people and the forest resource will run via some policy ideas or customs, activities and management .

Although the environmental aspects were not ignored nevertheless the emphasis has been to use the forest as commodity for timber products. There have been several historical instances of devastations of forests as a result of the overexploitation which resulted to become a threat to the local communities.

Most of the forest policies recognise the following functions:

- the production of wood and other forest products;
- the protection and conservation of the environment (soil, water, wildlife etc.); and
- the provision of opportunities for recreation.

During the last two decades shrinkage and degradation of forests mainly because of phenomenal increase in the biotic pressure in the developing countries and over consumption in the developed countries, has specially attracted the attention of the forest policies of different countries and the world as a whole.

The Forest Policies and the International Organisations have lately concentrated to resolve the following two historical issues which have assumed prolific dimension and are likely to be the potential challenges for forest management in the recent future.

First, there is an attempt to evolve a clear definition of the rights of ownership and use as a prerequisite for the conservation and management of forests, and, secondly,explain as to how the production and service functions can be maneuvered to best serve the needs of growing populations and diversifying societies.

Because of the phenomenal increase in the biotic pressure of human and livestock on limited forest resource beyond carrying capacity in the developing countries and excessive demands of products to meet the sky diving consumption levels in the developed countries, the role of the forest and forestry in any country or region will be settled by two poles, the forest resource, i.e. the potential supply on the one hand and the need by society for forest products and services, i.e. the demand on the other hand. Neither supply nor demand is static. The forest resource can be managed for the optimal supply as the forest resource limits the possibilities of supply. There is a need of change in the basic thrust in the forest policies towards conservation, increased production and provision for alternatives for products of excessive demand.

Keeping in view the growing forest-people interface linkages most of the Forest Policies of the world have recognised in theory that the forest resource is part of the national wealth; that there are the rights and the obligations of present and future generations in respect of the uses of the wealth; and that ownership, including private ownership, carries with certain obligations to society as well as the right of fair compensation. However in actual practice the success of implementation has been limited owing to the conflicts in different functions.

Since the Forest Policy basically deals with the use of land for forestry including all secondary activities, and the provision of products and services, the underlying aim being to balance the demand and supply of forest products and services, and as both these aspects affect the relations between forest policy and other policies, therefore, there is a global need for the coordination and integration of the forest policy with the other policies which affect environment. Any country's economic policy, social and environmental policies influence and get influenced by forest policy in a web of complicated and sometimes not very clearly visible interactions which change as societies and governments shift their priorities. During the 1980s, the involvement of the local people and the local settings of the various items have been recognised as the prime considerations of the forest policies.

4

Global View on Community Participation in Forestry

Forestry can play a significant role for the well-being of the people living in and around the forest areas in several ways. And conversely these people can play a major part in either making the forests around them more productive or gradually destroying. Some of the benefits to be derived by the rural people from forestry are the same in both developing and developed countries, for example forest products for domestic use, employment and income based on the forest as well as tourism. The policy implications are however considerably different. In developing countries the problems are both difficult and more urgent because of the majority of population are directly or indirectly dependent on forests, forest lands and forestry for basic necessities of life.

4.1 DEVELOPING COUNTRIES

'As deforestation progresses, it reduces the quality of life of millions of people in developing countries; their survival is threatened by the loss of the vegetation upon which they depend for their sources of household energy and many other goods. If tropical forests continue to be cleared at the current rate, at least 556 million acres (225 million hectares) will be cleared by the year 2000; if destruction of the tropical rain forests continues unabated, an estimated 10 to 20 per cent of the Earth's plant and animal life will be gone by the year 2000.

Reversing deforestation depends on political leadership and appropriate policy changes by developing-country governments to support community-level initiatives. The key ingredient is active participation by the millions of small farmers and landless people who daily use forests and trees to meet their needs'.

(World Commission on Environment and Development)

Successful forestry programmes in support of rural community development have been undertaken in a number of countries, in some cases with the assistance of international agencies and credit institutions. These countries include China, India, Indonesia, Philippines, Senegal, South Korea, and Upper Volta. Other countries are also shifting their attention for linking forestry with community development and revising their policies accordingly.

Community implies a fundamental change in a way of life that has remained almost constant for centuries, in fact a transition from the stone age to the 21th century. The problems associated with bringing out attitudinal changes and desired technological improvements have been addressed by most of the countries. Land reform and forestry extension have been identified as key components with respect to community development through forestry. It has been identified that although the question of land reform goes far beyond forest policy, but forestry and specially forestry in support of rural community development is profoundly affected by the system of land tenure. Regarding forestry extension, there has been emphasis on an effective extension service and incentives and also good collaboration between forestry extension and agricultural extension. One of the recent trends has been the promotion of tourism in forest areas intended to be in the best interests of the rural communities.

4.2 DEVELOPED COUNTRIES

'The industrialized world's demands for raw materials, high productivity, and material goods have imposed serious environmental impacts and high economic costs not only our countries, but also on the developing world. The existing international patterns of financial, economic, trade, and investment policies further add to the problems.

We must all be willing to examine our relations in international trade, investments, development assistance, industry, and agriculture in the light of the consequences these may have for underdevelopment and environmental destruction in the Third World. We must even be willing to go further and implement the means necessary to alleviate these symptoms'.

(World Commission on Environment and Development)

In most of the developed countries there was until very recently a steady migration of the population from the land to the towns which became even larger and more crowded while some tribal areas became more and more depopulated. The exodus from the country side has led to a shortage of forest workers in some areas, although mechanisation has greatly reduced manpower requirements in forestry as it has been done in farming.

Mechanisation of the forestry activities, forestry industries and the tourism have been the manifestations of the forest policies which have exercised influences on community development . In Western Europe considerable areas of land have been freed for afforestation. This helps to curb agricultural over-production and will eventually reduce the timber deficit, two very desirable objectives. Further, in many countries of Europe, communal forests belonging to local village local communities constitute a significant proportion of the country's forest estate and have been of great benefit to the communities concerned, supplying them with produce and furnishing revenue which helps to defray the costs of public works. However, the efforts of collective ownership have met with only minor success.

Co-operative forests exist mainly in countries with centrally planned economies, but their importance varies. They are common in Germany and Hungary where they accounted for about 25% in 80s. In Bulgaria, Romania and the then USSR the percentage lies between 2 and 8 while in Poland this category of ownership is almost completely absent. The co-operative forests are managed by the co-operatives in the same way in all the centrally planned economies, but the ownership differs somewhat from country to country for historic reasons.

4.3 INTERNATIONAL ORGANISATIONS

Although most forest policy decisions are taken at the national level and are determined by national factors, but international influences on national policies are gaining in importance in a world in which nations are becoming more and more interdependent. After the Second World War the interactions and exchange of ideas among the international organisations have strengthened for the forestry activities. There are several aspects to the international dimensions of the forestry; the establishment of a data base, the exchange of technical information, collaborative action including aid programmes and trade are among the more important international forestry linkages, Aid programmes and also global forestry issues like biodiversity conservation and wilderness heritage etc. attract the attention and involvement of the major international organisations. International actions may be particular to the forestry sector or the forestry components may be part of more general activities such as UNESCO's Man and Biosphere Programme, the United Nations Water Conference, Conference on the Desertification and United Nations Energy Conference, in all of which the role of forestry has emerged strongly to the forefront and given foresters an opportunity to present their case to much wider public.

The different international organisations relevant to forestry can be distinguished into following three categories :

4.3.1 World-wide Governmental Organisations

* F A O (Food and Agriculture Organisation of the UNO)
* U N E S C O (United Nations Education, Scientific and Cultural Organisation)
* U N C T A D (United Nations Conference on Trade and Development)
* U N I D O (United Nations Industrial Development Organisation)
* W M O (World Meteorological Organisation)
* I L O (International Labour Organisation)
* World Bank

4.3.2 World-wide Non Governmental Organisations

* I U F R O (International Union of Forestry Research Organisation)
* I U C N (International Union for the Conservation of Nature and Natural Resources)
* W W F (World Wildlife Fund)
* I C R A F (International Council for Research in Agroforestry)

4.3.3 Regional Organisations and Groups

* United Nations Regional Economic Commissions
  - E C E (The Economic Commission for Europe)
  - E C A (The Economic Commission for Africa)
  - E C L A (The Economic Commission for Latin America)
  - E S C A P (The Economic and Social Commission for Asia and the Pacific)
  - E C W A (The Economic Commission for Western Asia)
* O E C D (Organisation for Economic Co-operation and Development)
* E E C (European Economic Community)
* Regional Development Banks
  - The African Development Bank
  - The Inter-American Development Bank
  - The Asian Development Bank
  - The Caribbean Development Bank

4.3.4 Regional Groups

* Nordic Forestry Union (Denmark, Finland, Iceland, Norway, Sweden)
* European Alpine Countries Association
* Confederation Europeanne d'Agriculture
* Council of Europe

* Centre for European Policy Studies
* Commonwealth Forestry Institute
* Commonwealth Forestry Bureau
* Commonwealth Forestry Conference
* World Forestry Congress

Some of these organisations are directly or indirectly linked and involved with the forestry based community development and have lately formulated guidelines / frameworks for forestry - community linkages.

The objectives and programmes of various related organisations relevant to forestry linked community development are cited here.

4.4 F A O

4.4.1 Sub Programmes of FAO Forestry Programme

4.4.1.1 Forest Resources and Environment

Sub-objective b : 'Expansion of forest tree plantations for environmental protection and as renewable sources of energy, timber, fodder, and food, giving special emphasis to drought resistant tree species that can directly support *rural development* while also providing fuelwood; continuation of programmes of :

- quality forest seed collection and distribution,
- forest genetic resources conservation and use'.

4.4.1.2 Forest Industries and Trade

Sub-objective a : 'Assist member countries to build up the forest industries sector necessary for maximising the contribution that forest resources can make to economic and social development, specially *rural areas*.

Sub-objective b ii : 'The promotion of investment in the improvement of existing industries in *rural areas* and the establishment of additional ones, both at the village and larger *community levels.*

4.4.1.3 Forest Investments and Institutions

Sub-objective d : 'Provide international statistical information with respect to resource, capacity, production, trade and manpower in the forest sector, giving special attention to information gaps related to statistical indicators of *rural development* in the forest sector.

4.4.1.4 Forestry and Rural Development

Sub-objectives

a. Identification and development of *community* level systems which enable *rural people* to best meet those of their needs which are based on forest outputs.
b. Strengthening of government and non- government institutions which support and service rural forestry activities.
c. Establishment of land - use systems which integrate trees and agriculture in a manner which is both environmentally sound and optimally productive for *rural people.*
d. Identification and promotion of off-farm *rural employment* and income generating activities in forestry.
e. Monitoring of fuelwood supply and demand imbalances.

4.4.2 FAO Action Plan

Further FAO has identified the role of the communities in the development of forest resource under section 5.8 of the Tropical Forestry Action Plan under the following head :

Organisation of Rural Communities for Forestry Development

4.4.2.1 Background

It is generally recognised that the organisation of the rural people with a view to solving their problems and defending their common rights is extremely important. The task of the forestry sector to maintain or recover the right of these communities to have access to the natural resources, which are essential for their subsistence, has not received sufficient attention. The frequent depletion of the natural forests, often sanctioned by law, has separated man from the forest, thus leading to a degradation of the resource. Also, many forest development strategies of the past did not recognise the benefits rural communities should derive from the forests through their participation in the development activities. As it is important to protect forest resources, action must be taken to organise rural populations in such away that they can contribute to forestry activities in a conjunction with public or private agencies.

4.4.2.2 Objectives

i. to develop incentives to encourage participation in forestry;
ii. to promote rural organisations such as associations, cooperatives, etc.;
iii. to promote the integration of rural organisations with forestry activities being carried out by public or private entities;
iv. to develop appropriate forestry training programmes for rural people;
v. to develop forestry extension programmes.

4.4.2.3 Activities

i. review or modify legal instruments related to forestry and rural incentives;
ii. carry out socio-cultural studies on the rural communities in forest zones;

iii. set up rural organisations programmes for forestry activities in conjunction with public or private entities dealing this subject;
iv. establish a pilot project for rural community participation in forestry development;
v. seek technical and financial assistance to support and improve field activities of rural organisations;
vi. find appropriate mechanisms for the distribution and marketing of forest products produced by rural organisations.

The FAO has released elaborate guidelines and recommendations on people's participation in rural development and criteria and indicators of sustainable forest management, (FAO 1992 & 1996).

4.5 UNESCO

Promote self reliance among countries of the humid and sub - humid tropics in research and management and to encourage the continuing *participation* of various sectors of the *community* in these activities.

4.6 UNEP

Promote world or *regional* interest in major *environmental subjects* and an integrated approach to them.

4.7 ILO

Training of *Forest workers*, where it shares the secretariat responsibility with other participating organisations.

4.8 WORLD BANK

Change in forestry programmes with special reference to the role of forests in *rural development* and environment particularly watershed-protection.

4.9 WORLD FOOD PROGRAMME

Distribution of food aid to developing countries for labour intensive projects including Forestry Projects for *rural development.*

4.10 EEC

4.10.1 Objectives and principles of EEC forestry policy

1.6 Forestry policy measures should be coordinated at *community level* to the extent to achieve common objectives.

2.3 Woodlands should not be regarded as land reserves but in their own right on the basis of all the products and services that forest provide to the *community.*

3.1 Regional Development and the living standards of rural populations, specially in less favored areas.

Increased wood production can make to cover the *community's requirements* of wood.

7.4 Promotion at *community level* of selected research projects of particular importance and beyond the capacity of individual national effort.

5

Community Participation Reflections of Earth Summit and Agenda 21

5.1 TOKYO DECLARATION-ADOPTION OF AGREEMENTS ON ENVIRONMENT AND DEVELOPMENT

'....In order to associate fully the private sector in the implementation of Agenda 21, it would be useful to set up an instrument for coordinating the *participation* of firms, non-governmental organisations and *private persons* into the planning, the financing and the realization of environmental actions linked to *local* development projects'.

5.2 INAUGURAL SPEECH-UNCED CONFERENCE ON ENVIRONMENT AND DEVELOPMENT –UN SECRETARY GENERAL BUOTROS-GHALI

'....The World Conference of *Indigenous People* met to share their experience and concerns. They are repositories of much of the *traditional knowledge* and wisdom from which modernisation has separated most of us. They are *custodians*, too, of some of world's most important and vulnerable ecosystems – tropical forests, desert and arctic regions. We must hear and heed their voices, learn from their experience and respect their right to live in their own lands in accordance with their traditions, values and cultures'.

5.3 UNEP CONVENTION ON BIOLOGICAL DIVERSITY – 5 JUNE 1992

5.3.1 Preamble

'....Recognising the close and traditional dependence of many indigenous and local communities embodying traditional lifestyles on biological resources, and the desirability of sharing equitably benefits arising from the use of traditional knowledge, innovations and practices relevant to the conservation of biological diversity and the sustainable use of its components'.

5.3.2 Article 8 : In-situ Conservation

'....Subject to its national legislation, respect, preserve and maintain knowledge, innovations and practices of indigenous and local communities embodying traditional lifestyles relevant for the conservation and sustainable use of biological diversity and promote their wider application with the approval and involvement of the holders of such knowledge, innovations and practices and encourage equitable sharing arising from the utilization of such knowledge, innovations and practices'.

5.3.3 Article 18-Impact Assessment and Minimizing Adverse Impacts

'1 a. Each contracting party, as far as possible and as appropriate, shall : introduce appropriate procedures requiring environmental impact assessment of its proposed projects that are likely to have significant adverse effects on biological diversity with a view to avoiding or minimizing such effects and, where appropriate, allow for public participation in such procedures'.

5.4 Forest Principles -13 Jusne 1992

Adoption of Agreements on Environment and Development :

Nonlegally Binding Authoritative Statement of Principles for a Conservation and Sustainable Development of All Types of Forests.

'2 d....Government should promote and provide opportunities for the participation of the interested parties, including local communities and indigenous people, industries, labour, non-governmental organizations and individuals, forest dwellers and women, in the development, implementation and planning of national forest policies'.

'5 a....National Forest policies should recognize and duly support the identity, culture and the rights of indigenous people, their communities and other communities and forest dwellers. Appropriate conditions should be promoted for these groups to enable them to have an economic stake in forest use, perform economic activities, and achieve and maintain cultural identity and social organisation, as well as adequate levels of livelihood and well-being, through *inter alia*, those land tenure arrangements which serve as incentives for the sustainable management of forests'.

'6 d....The role of planted forests and permanent agricultural crops as sustainable and environmentally sound sources of renewable energy and industrial raw material should be recognised, enhanced and promoted. Their contribution to the maintenance of ecological processes, to offsetting pressure on primary/old-growth forest and to providing regional employment and development with the adequate involvement of local inhabitants should be recognised and enhanced'.

'9 b....The problems that hinder efforts to attain the conservation and sustainable use of forest resources and that stem from the lack of alternative options available to local communities, in particular the urban poor and poor rural populations who are economically and socially dependent on the forest and forest resources, should be addressed by the Governments and the international community'.

'12 d....Appropriate indigenous capacity and local knowledge regarding the conservation and sustainable development of forest should, through institutional and financial support, and in collaboration with the people in the local communities concerned, be recognised, respected, recorded, developed and, as appropriate, introduced in the implementation of programmes. Benefits arising from the utilization of indigenous knowledge should therefore be equitably shared with such people'.

5.5 THE RIO DECLARATION ON ENVIRONMENT AND DEVELOPMENT–ADOPTION OF AGREEMENTS ON ENVIRONMENT AND DEVELOPMENT

5.5.1 Principle 10

'....Environmental issues are best handled with the participation of all concerned citizens, at the relevant level. At the national level, each individual shall have appropriate access to information concerning the environment that is held by public authorities, including information on hazardous materials and activities in their communities, and the opportunity to participate in decision-making processes. States shall facilitate and encourage public awareness and participation by making information widely available. Effective access to judicial and administrative proceedings, including redress and remedy, shall be provided'.

5.5.2 Principle 22

'....*Indigenous people* and their *communities*, and other *local communities,* have a vital role in environmental management and development because of their knowledge and traditional practices. States should recognize and duly support their identity, culture and interests and enable their effective *participation* in the achievement of *sustainable* development'.

5.6 AGENDA 21

5.6.1 Chapter 3–Combating Poverty

'(a) *Empowering communities* : 3.7....Sustainable development must be achieved at every level of society. People's organisations, women's groups and non-governmental organisations are important sources of innovation and action at the local level and have a strong interest and proven ability to promote sustainable livelihoods. Governments in cooperation with appropriate international and non-governmental organisations, should support a community-driven approach to sustainability, which would include, *inter alia* :

a. empowering women through full participation in decision making;
b. respecting the cultural integrity and the rights of indigenous people and their communities;
c. promoting or establishing grass-roots mechanisms to allow for the sharing of experience and knowledge between communities;
d. giving communities a large measure of participation in the sustainable management and protection of the local natural resources in order to enhance their productive capacity;
e. establishing a network of community-based learning centres for capacity-building and sustainable development'.

'(b) *Management related activities* - 3.8....Governments, with the assistance of and in cooperation with appropriate international, non-governmental and local community organizations, should establish measures that will directly or indirectly :

d. empower community organizations and people to enable them to achieve sustainable livelihoods;
h. establish new community-based mechanisms and strengthen existing mechanisms to enable communities to gain sustained access to resources needed by the poor to overcome their poverty;

e. implement mechanisms for popular participation – particularly by poor people, especially women – in local community groups, to promote sustainable development'.

5.6.2 Chapter 7 : Promoting Sustainable Human Settlement Development

'7.20 g....*Empower community* groups, non-governmental organizations and *individuals* to assume the *authority* and responsibility for managing and enhancing their immediate environment through participatory tools, techniques and approaches embodied in the concept of environmental care'.

5.6.3 Chapter 8 : Integrating Environment and Development in Decision Making

'(a) *Improving decision making process* : 8.4 f....Ensuring access by the *public* to relevant information *facilitating* the reception of *public views* and allowing for effective *participation*'.

'(b) Improving planning and management systems : 8.5h ....Establishing *procedures* for *involving local communities* in contingency planning for environmental and industrial accidents, and maintaining an open exchange of information on local hazards'.

5.6.4 Chapter 10 : Integrated Approach to the Planning and Management of Land Resources

'10.5....Protected areas, private property rights, the rights of indigenous people and their communities and other local communities and the economic role of women in agriculture and rural development, among other issues, should be taken account.

(d) To create mechanisms to facilitate the active involvement and participation of all concerned, particularly communities and people at the local level, in decision-making on land use and management, by not later than 1996'.

'10.10....Government at the appropriate level, in collaboration with national organisations and with the support of regional and international organizations, should establish innovative procedures, programmes, projects and services that facilitate and encourage the active participation of those affected in the decision making and implementation process, especially of groups that have, hitherto, often been excluded, such as women, youth, indigenous people and their communities and other local communities'.

5.6.5 Chapter 11 - Combating Deforestation

'11.1....More effective measures and approaches are often required at the national level to improve and harmonize policy formulation, planning and programming; legislative measures and instruments; development patterns; *participation* of general public, especially women and *indigenous people;* involvement of youth; roles of private sector, local organizations non-governmental organizations and cooperatives; development of technical and multidisciplinary skills and quality of human resources; forestry extension and public education; research capability and support; administrative structures and mechanisms, including intersectoral coordination, decentralization and responsibility and incentive systems; and dissemination of information and public relations'.

'11.4 b....Promoting *participation* of the private sector, labour unions, rural cooperatives, local communities, indigenous people, youth, women, user groups and non-governmental organizations in forest-related activities, and access to information and training programmes within the national context;

'11.12....The greening of suitable areas, in all its component activities, is an effective way of increasing public awareness and participation in protecting and managing forest resource'.

'11.14....Governments, with the participation of the private sector, non-governmental organizations, local community groups, indigenous people, women, local government units and the public at large, should act to maintain and expand the existing vegetative cover wherever ecologically, socially and economically feasible, through technical cooperation and other forms of support.

i....Launching or improving opportunities for participation of all people, including youth, women, indigenous people and local communities in the formulation, development and implementation of forest-related programmes and other activities, taking due account of the local needs and cultural values'.

'11.31 a....To strengthen or establish systems for the assessment and systematic observations of forests and forests land with a view to assessing the impacts of programmes, projects and activities on the quality and extent of forest resources, land available for afforestation, and land tenure, and to integrate the systems in a continuing process of research and in-depth analysis, while ensuring necessary modifications and improvements for planning and decision-making.

Specific emphasis should be given to the *participation of rural people* in these processes'.

5.6.6 Chapter 12 : Combating Desertification and Drought

'12.14 b....Promote the *involvement of the local population,* particularly women and youth, in the collection and utilization of environmental information through education and awareness-building'.

'12.17 a....As regards areas not yet affected or only slightly affected by desertification, to ensure appropriate management of existing natural formations (including forests) for the conservation of biodiversity, watershed protection, sustainability of their production and agricultural development, and other purposes, with the *full participation of indigenous people'.*

'12.18 e....Promote *participatory management* of natural resources, including rangeland, to meet both the needs of rural populations and conservation purposes, based on innovative or adapted *indigenous technologies'*.

'12.28 f....Develop infrastructure, as well as local production and marketing capacity, by *involving the local people* to promote alternative livelihood systems and alleviate poverty'.

'12.29 b....Conduct inventory of natural resources (soil, water and vegetation) and their state of degradation, based primarily on technical packages of the *local population* (e.g., rapid rural appraisal)'.

'12.55....it is necessary to go beyond the theoretical ideal of popular participation and to focus on obtaining *actual active popular involvement,* rooted in the concept of partnership. This implies the *sharing* of responsibilities and the mutual involvement of all parties'.

'12.56 d....To support *local communities* in their own efforts in combating desertification, and to draw on the knowledge and experience of the populations concerned, ensuring the *full participation* of women and *indigenous populations'*.

'12.57 c....Define specific programme / project objectives in cooperation *with local communities;* design *local management plans* to include such measures of progress, thereby providing a means of altering project design or changing management practices, as appropriate'.

'f....Develop training programmes to increase the level of education and *participation of people,* particularly women and *indigenous groups,* through, *inter alia*, literacy and the development of technical skills'.

5.6.7 Chapter 13 : Management Fragile Ecosystems: Sustainable Mountain Development

'13.14....Promoting integrated watershed development programmes through effective *participation of local people* is a key to preventing further ecological imbalance'.

'13.16 h....Undertake the management related activities, taking into account the need full *participation of* women, including *indigenous people and local communities*, in development'.

5.6.8 Chapter 15 : Conservation of Biological Diversity

'15.3....Effective national action and international cooperation are required for the *in situ* protection of ecosystems, for the *ex situ* conservation of biological and genetic resources and the enhancement of ecosystem functions. The *participation* and support of the *local communities* are elements essential to the success of such an approach'.

'15.4....Governments at the appropriate level, with the cooperation of the relevant United Nations bodies and regional, inter-governmental and non-governmental organizations, the private sector and financial institutions, and taking into consideration *indigenous people and their communities,* as well as social and economic factors, should :

g....Recognize and foster the traditional methods and the knowledge of *indigenous people and their communities,* emphasizing the particular role of women, relevant to the conservation of biological diversity and the sustainable use of biological resources, and ensure the opportunity for the *participation* of those groups in the economic and commercial benefits derived from the use of such *traditional* methods and knowledge'.

'15.5....Governments at the appropriate levels, consistent with national policies and practices, with the cooperation of the relevant United Nations bodies and, as appropriate, inter-governmental organizations and with the support of *indigenous people* and their communities, non-governmental organizations and other groups, including the business and scientific communities, and consistent with the requirements of international law, should, as appropriate:

e....Subject to national legislation, taken action to respect, record protect and promote the wider application of the knowledge, innovations and practices of *indigenous and local communities* embodying traditional lifestyles for the conservation of biological diversity and the sustainable use of biological resources, with a view to the fair and equitable sharing of the benefits arising, and promote mechanisms to involve those communities, including women, in the conservation and management of ecosystems;

'f....The work should be undertaken with the widest possible participation, especially of *indigenous people and their communities,* including women'.

'15.6....Governments at the appropriate levels, consistent with national policies and practices, with the cooperation of the relevant United Nations bodies and, as appropriate, inter-governmental organizations and with the support of *indigenous people* and their communities, non-governmental organizations and other groups, including the business and scientific communities, and consistent with the requirements of international law, should, as appropriatc:

c....Initiate or further develop methodologies and begin or continue work on surveys at the appropriate level on the status of ecosystems and establish baseline information on biological and genetic resources, including those in terrestrial, aquatic, coastal and marine ecosystems, as well as inventories undertaken with the participation of local and indigenous people and their communities;

f....Collect, assess and make available relevant and reliable information in a timely manner and in a form suitable for decision-making at all levels, with the full support and participation of local and indigenous people and their communities'.

'15.11....Enhance the capacity of governmental and private institutions, at the appropriate level, responsible for protected area planning and management to undertake intersectoral coordination and planning with other governmental institutions, non-governmental organizations and, where appropriate, indigenous people and their communities'.

5.6.9 Chapter 23 : Strengthening the Role of Major Groups

'23.2....One of the fundamental prerequisites for the achievement of sustainable development is broad *participation in decision-making.* Furthermore, in the more specific context of environment and development, the need for new forms of participation has emerged. This includes the need of *individuals, groups and organizations to participate* in environmental impact assessment procedures and to know about and *participate in decisions,* particularly those which potentially affect the communities in which they live and work. Individuals, groups and organizations should have access to information relevant to environment and development held by national authorities, including information on products and activities that have or are likely to have a significant impact on the environment, and information on environmental protection measures'.

5.6.10 Chapter 26 : Recognising and Strengthening the Role of Indigenous People and their communities

'26.1....In view of the inter-relationship between the natural environment and its sustainable development and the cultural, social, economic and physical well-being of *indigenous people,* national and international efforts to implement environmentally sound and sustainable development should recognize, accommodate, promote and strengthen the *role of indigenous people and communities'.*

'26.3 a....Establishment of a process to empower indigenous people and their communities through measures that include :

i. Adoption or strengthening of appropriate policies and / or legal instruments at the national level;

ii. Recognition that the lands of indigenous people and their communities should be protected from activities that are environmentally unsound or that the indigenous people concerned consider to be socially and culturally inappropriate;

iii. Recognition of their values, traditional knowledge and resource management practices with a view to promoting environmentally sound and sustainable development;

iv. Recognition that traditional and direct dependence on renewable resources and ecosystems, including sustainable harvesting, continues to be essential to the cultural, economic and physical well-being of indigenous people and their communities;

v. Development and strengthening of national dispute-resolution arrangements in relation to settlement of land and resource-management concerns;

vi. Support for alternative environmentally sound means of production to ensure a range of choices on how to improve their quality of life so that they effectively participate in sustainable development;

vii. Enhancement of capacity-building for indigenous communities, based on the adaptation and exchange of traditional experience, knowledge and resource-management practices, to ensure their sustainable development;

b....Establishment, where appropriate, of arrangements to strengthen the active participation of indigenous people and their communities in the national formulation of policies, laws and programmes relating to resource management and other development processes that may affect them, and their initiation of proposals for such policies and programmes;

c....Involvement of indigenous people and their communities at the national and local levels in resource management and conservation strategies and other relevant programmes established to support and review sustainable development strategies, such as those suggested in other programme areas of Agenda 21'.

'26.4....Some indigenous people and their communities may require, in accordance with national legislation, greater control over their lands, self management of their resources, participation in development decisions affecting them, including wherever appropriate, participation in the establishment or management of protected areas. The following are some of the specific measures which Government could take :

a. Consider the ratification and application of existing international conventions relevant to indigenous people and their communities (where not yet done) and provide support for the adoption by the General Assembly of a declaration on indigenous rights;

b. Adopt or strengthen appropriate policies and / or legal instruments that will protect indigenous intellectual and cultural property and right to preserve customary and administrative systems and practices'.

26.5....United Nations Organizations and other international development and finance organizations and Governments should, drawing on the active participation of indigenous people and their communities, as appropriate, take the following measures, *inter alia*, to incorporate their values, views and knowledge, including the unique contribution of indigenous women, in resource management and other policies and programmes that may affect them :

a. Appoint a special focal point within each international organization, and organize annual interorganizational coordination meetings in consultation with Governments and indigenous organizations, as appropriate, and develop a procedure within and between operational agencies for assisting Governments in ensuring the coherent and coordinated incorporation of the views of indigenous people in the design and implementation of policies and programmes. Under this procedure, indigenous people and their communities should be informed and consulted and allowed to participate in national decision-making, in particular regarding regional and international cooperative efforts. In addition, these policies and programmes should take fully into account strategies based on indigenous initiatives;

b. Provide technical and financial assistance for capacity-building programme to support the sustainable self-development of indigenous people and their communities;

c. Strengthen research and education programmes aimed at :
   i. Achieving a better understanding of indigenous people's knowledge and management experience related to the environment, and applying this to contemporary development challenges;
   ii. Increasing the efficiency of indigenous peoples' resource management systems, for example, by promoting the adaptation and dissemination of suitable technological innovations;

d. Contribute to the endeavours of indigenous people and their communities in resource management and conservation strategies (such as those that may be developed under appropriate projects funded through the Global Environmental Facility and Tropical Forestry Action Plan) and other Programme areas of Agenda 21, including programmes to collect, analyse and use data and other information in support of sustainable development projects'.

'26.6....Governments, in full partnership with indigenous people and their communities should, where appropriate :

a. Develop or strengthen national arrangements to consult with indigenous people and their communities with a view to reflecting their needs and incorporating their values and traditional and other knowledge and practices in national policies and programmes in the field of natural resource management and conservation and other development programmes affecting them;
b. Cooperate at regional level, where appropriate, to address common indigenous issues with a view to recognising and strengthening their participation in sustainable development'.

'26.8....Governments should incorporate, in *collaboration* with the *indigenous people* affected, the *rights and responsibilities of indigenous people and their communities* in the legislation of each country, suitable to the country's specific situation. Developing countries may require technical assistance to implement these activities'.

'26.9....International development agencies and Government should commit financial and other resources to education and training for *indigenous people and their communities* to develop their capacities to achieve their sustainable development, and to contribute to and *participate* in sustainable and *equitable development* at the national level. Particular attention should be given to strengthening the role of indigenous women'.

5.6.11 Chapter 32 : Strengthening the Role of Farmers

'32.6 a....To encourage a *decentralised decision-making* process through the creation and strengthening of local and village organizations that would delegate power and responsibility to *primary users of natural resources*'.

5.6.12 Chapter 34 : Transfer of Environmentally Sound Technology Cooperation and Capacity-Building

'34.14 c....To facilitate the maintenance and promotion of environmentally sound *indigenous technologies* that may have been neglected or displaced, in particular in developing countries, paying particular attention to their priority needs and taking into account the complementary roles of men and women'.

5.6.13 Chapter 35 : Science for Sustainable Development

'35.6 d....The generation and application of knowledge, especially *indigenous and local knowledge,* to the capacities of different environments and cultures, to achieve sustained levels of development, taking into account interrelationship at the national, regional and international levels;

f....*Participation of people* in setting priorities and in decision-making relating to sustainable development'.

'35.21 a....Education, training and facilities for local research and development and human resource development in basic scientific disciplines and in environment-related sciences, utilizing where appropriate, *traditional and local knowledge of sustainability;*

d....Improving access to relevant information for scientists and decision makers, with aim of improving *public awareness and participation* in decision-making'.

5.6.14 Chapter 36 : Promoting Education, Public Awareness and Training

'36.10 a....Countries should strengthen existing advisory bodies to establish new ones for public environment and development information, and should coordinate activities with, among others, the United Nations, non-governmental organizations and important media. They should encourage public participation in discussions of environmental policies and assessments. Governments should also facilitate and support national to local networking of information through existing networks;

f....Countries, in cooperation with scientific community, should establish ways of employing modern communication technologies for effective public outreach. National and local educational authorities and relevant United Nations agencies should expand, as appropriate, the use of audio-visual methods, especially in rural areas in mobile units, by producing television and radio programmes for developing countries, involving local participation, employing interactive multimedia methods with folk media'.

5.6.15 Chapter 40 : Information for Decision-Making

'40.11....Countries, with the cooperation with international organizations, should establish supporting mechanisms to provide *local communities* and resource users with the information and know-how they need to manage their environment and resources sustainability, applying *traditional and indigenous knowledge* and approaches when appropriate. This is particularly relevant for rural and urban populations and indigenous, women's and youth groups'.

6

Community Participation in Forestry in Australia

The excerpts of relevant sections envisaging community participation and forestry under various forestry acts, policies and other documents have been quoted here to understand the process of community participation in forest management.

6.1 FORESTRY ACT 1920

6.1.1 Forestry Amendment (Forestry Corporation) Bill 1993

'Public access to State Forest–
20 B (1)....The corporation may exercise its power so as to afford members of public access to State forest for such recreational purposes as are not incompatible with the management of State forest under this Act'.

'Forest Management Plans to be made available for public inspection–
22K (1)....The corporation must, at all reasonable times, make each –

a. draft of a proposed forest management plan;
b. interim forest management plan; and
c. forest management plan–

available for public inspection at its main office, and must, upon request, provide a copy of that plan to any person.

(2) The corporation may charge a fee for providing a copy of that plan under subsection (1) but such fee is not to exceed the reasonable cost of providing the copy.

6.2 NATIONAL FOREST POLICY STATEMENT

'Foreword....This statement has been *jointly* developed by the Commonwealth, States and territories through the Australian Forestry Council and the Australian and New Zealand Environment and Conservation Council in consultation with other relevant government agencies, the Australian Local Government Association, Unions, industry representatives, conservation organizations and the *general community'*.

'1. *Introduction*....This Statement provides a framework within which pressures for change can be identified and accommodated so as to ensure that the Australian *community* derives optimal benefit from its forest and forest resources'. (pp. 2)

'2. *The Vision*....This vision has a number of characteristics :

* There is a 'holistic' approach to managing forests for all their values and uses so as to optimise *benefits to the community.*
* Forest management is effective and *responsive to the community.*
* The Australian *community* will have a sound understanding of the values of forests and sustainable forest management, and *will participate* in *decision-making process* relating to forest use and management'. (pp. 3)

'3. *National Goals*....Public awareness, education and *involvement*: The goals are to foster community understanding of and support for ecologically sustainable forest management in Australia and to provide opportunities for *effective public participation in decision making'*. (pp. 6)

'4.1 *Conservation*....The development of the management plans will incorporate *community consultations'*. (pp. 11)

'4.2 *Wood production and industry development*....Prices will be market based, at least cover the full cost of efficient management (including regeneration) attributable to wood production, include a fair return on capital, and provide an adequate *return to the community from the use of a public* resource'. (pp. 20)

'....Where competitive markets are not achievable, prices set through administratively determined allocation systems should at least cover the efficient costs of wood production and provide an adequate *return to the community'*. (pp. 21)

'....Governments have a shared responsibility to ensure that the *community receives the optimum return* from all uses of public native forests. This involves two aspects of management of those forests : first, meeting community service obligations such as providing recreation access and facilities, and meeting other social and conservation objectives; second, managing forests for commercial products and uses'. (pp. 21)

'4.3 *Inter-governmental arrangements*....State processes are well established, and they are periodically reviewed to take account of *community priorities'*.

'....At the operational level, the States will ensure that management agencies, consulting with local government, regional organisations and other authorities as appropriate and providing opportunities for *public consultation'*.

'4.4 *Plantations*....With *appropriate public involvement*, the State Governments will pursue planning policies that provide zoning suitable for commercial planting on private lands and give security to that zoning framework, tree planting and subsequent harvesting for commercial wood production will be an 'as of right' use'.

'4.9 *Public awareness, education and involvement....*Forest management agencies manage public forests on behalf of the *community.* It is important that these agencies be *accountable to the community* for their stewardship of the community's assets.

It is equally important to foster community understanding of and support for ecologically sustainable forest management, by providing greater *opportunities for the community* to obtain information about forest ecology, the management of Australia's forests, and forests' nature conservation, heritage, and economic and wood production values. This will enable the community to make a more considered contribution within the land use decision-making process and to forest management issues.

Accordingly, the Governments' strategy will involve the following:

* provision to the *community of information* about forests and forest management;
* continued support for the establishment of forest information facilities, such as demonstration forests and visitor information centres;
* continued development by the States of comprehensive and publicly available forest management plans based on extensive public consultation and advanced planning techniques'. (pp. 38)

'*Glossary – Ecologically Sustainable Development* : There is no common definition in the literature for the term 'ecologically sustainable development'. In considering this issue, the Ecologically Sustainable Group on forest use specified three requirements for sustainable forest use : maintaining the ecological processes within forests (the formation of soil, energy flows, and the carbon, nutrient and water cycles); maintaining the biological diversity of forests; and *optimising the benefits to the community from all uses of forests* within ecological constraints. The National Forest Policy Statement adopts these principles as the basis for ecologically sustainable development'. (pp. 47)

6.3 LAND USE PLANNING AND APPROVALS ACT 1993

6.3.1 State Policies and Projects Act 1993

'Sustainable Development Objectives of the Resource Management and planning System of Tasmania – Schedule 1 – part 1

c. to encourage public involvement in resource management and planning;

e. to promote the sharing of responsibility for resource management and planning between the different spheres of Government, the community and industry in the State.'

6.4 REGIONAL FOREST AGREEMENT FOR TASMANIA

'A Regional Forest Agreement (RFA) is an agreement between a State and the Commonwealth Government which covers aspects of forest resource allocation, conservation and management.

Under the National Forest Policy Statement signed by Tasmania in April 1995, the Tasmanian and Commonwealth governments agreed to a framework and a joint scientific and public consultation process for a comprehensive regional assessment of forest leading to negotiation of a Regional Forest Agreement for Tasmania.

To assist in developing the process and timetable for the development of a RFA for Tasmania, a Scoping Agreement was signed by both governments in January 1996. The Scoping Agreement deals with Tasmania as a single region and includes both public and private forested lands. It outlines that the RFA is to provide for long-term ecologically sustainable management of forests and development of competitive and efficient forest industries'.

6.4.1 Public Consultation and Development of the Tasmanian RFA

'Tasmanian and Commonwealth governments are jointly responsible for all natural, social and cultural assessments contributing to the

RFA process (Figure 6.1). In recognition that effective community involvement is critical to the successful completion and enduring life of the RFA, public consultation will be a feature of the development of all facets of the RFA. The Tasmanian and Commonwealth governments are using the Tasmanian Public Land Use Commission (PLUC) Inquiry Process as the primary vehicle for public consultation and discussion'.

6.4.2 Consultation Process

The PLUC public consultation process provides for public participation in three distinct stages : first, input to the Terms of Reference for the Inquiry; secondly, an information gathering stage (Background Reports); and thirdly, in the development of options stage (Proposed Recommendations Report). The information gathering stage includes all relevant biophysical, social, cultural and economic issues and provides an opportunity for the information base to be modified, clarified or corrected through public consultation prior to participation in the development of options stage. To assist in the complex task of presenting and consulting on the wide ranging matters to be dealt with in the background Reports, a number of (probably three) Background Reports will be published for leading up to the Scoping Agreement and the methodologies proposed to be used to collect the relevant comprehensive regional assessment (CRA) information, the second on the environmental and heritage CRA facts of the matter and the third on the social and economic CRA facts of the matter.

The consultation process is both wide-ranging and participatory through release of inquiry reports as well as opportunities for carefully focused issue-specific consultation for those key matters requiring special attention. Feedback is an integral part of the consultation process, mainly via acknowledgements of how information emanating from the public consultation process has been used in the development of options. Publication of consultation analysis reports is also proposed. Workshops with community groups are organised for key inputs to the information in the

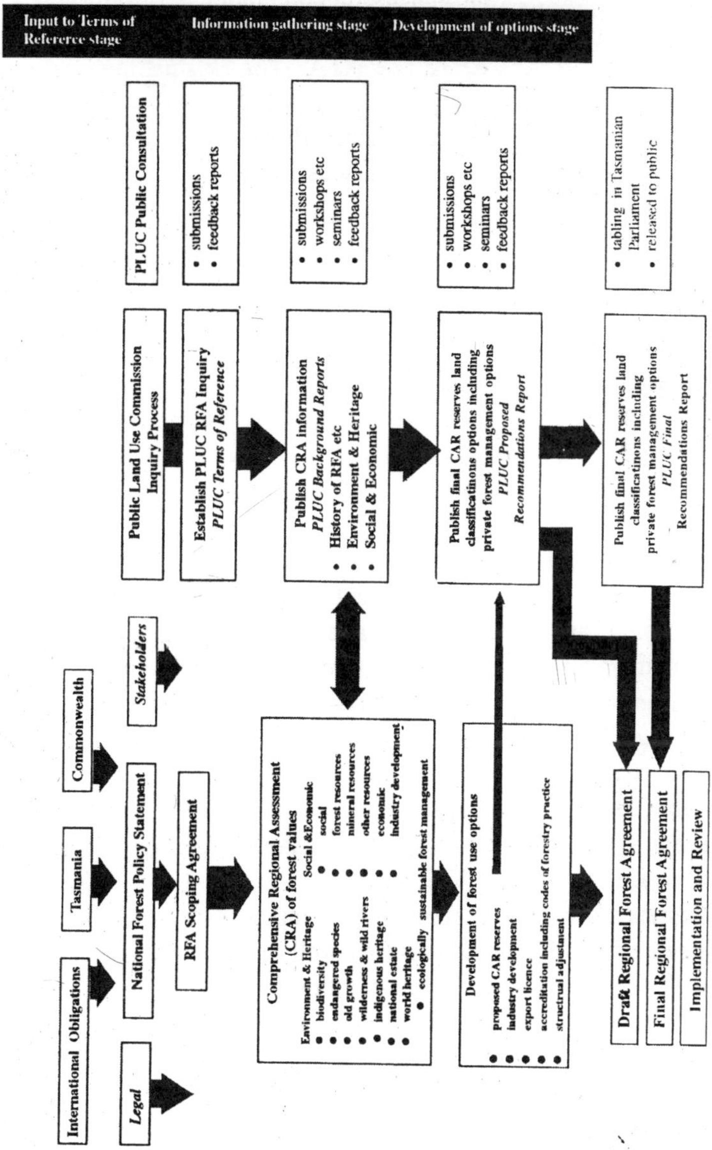

Fig. 6.1 : Regional Forest Agreement Process : Tasmania

Background Reports as well as during the development of options stage. Based on the specific issues which emerge from public consultation, forums and workshops at appropriate locations and venues, the Agreement is developed.

6.4.3 Involvement in consultation process

There are multiple stages for public participation in the development of the RFA. Each of the Background Papers and the Proposed Recommendations Reports will be announced in the Public Notices Section of the Examiner, Advocate, Mercury and Australian newspapers. Media reports will also announce key stages of the inquiry. Information also will be shared through an occasional information sheet series and brochures.

6.4.4 Public Participation in the Integration Process for RFA

6.4.4.1 Invitation

An invitation is extended to persons or groups interested in the use and management of Tasmania's forests to participate in the RFA integration process. This process will involve the development of options for forest conservation, forest use and industry development that may be applied to Tasmania's public forests in the Tasmanian Regional Forest Agreement.

Forests on private land will also be addressed under the RFA. The identification of draft RFA management options for private forested land involves a separate consultation process facilitated by the Public Land Use Commission.

6.4.4.2 Information

A comprehensive pool of information is being assembled through a range of studies on the environmental, heritage, social, and economic features of Tasmania's forests and resources and values. These studies were outlined in Commission's Inquiry Background Report Part A. The approaches taken in the studies are described in detail in the published supplement to the Background Report and were the subject of public workshops.

The results of many of the studies published as Background Report Parts describe the results of key environment and heritage studies and the results of the social and economic studies.

The integration process involves consideration of the results of these studies to develop a balanced RFA.

The main information products of the environmental and heritage assessments will be presented as tables, maps, and map overlays, derived from electronically stored data on a computerised Geographical Information System (GIS).

The main information products from the social and economic assessments will be presented as tables which will be supplemented by some maps. These products will assist in the identification of issues and in offering suggestions to address them.

A further part of the Background Report will be published for public comment and will cover a revues of forest management systems (described as the ecologically sustainable forest management assessment systems in background Report A). This is explained more fully in information Sheet no. 8 available from the Commission.

6.4.5 Framework

The forest conservation, forest use and industry development elements of the final RFA will be in accord with the framework established by the National Forest Policy Statement, the Tasmanian RFA Scoping Agreement , and other relevant policy documents agreed by the Tasmanian and Commonwealth Governments. The most useful contributions will be those that are in accord with this framework.

Members of the public may be interested in contributing in a range of ways, including presenting views, identifying issues and suggesting options for consideration in the integration process. Specific interests of individuals or groups may relate to parts or to all of Tasmania.

6.4.6 Organisations of Public Participation

The PLUC will assist the public to participate in the integration process. Assistance will include providing information, including tables ad maps, providing meeting venues, and access to computer facilities where appropriate.

The most efficient use of time and resource will be for participants to form themselves into groups which reflect a common interest. These groups will be given priority by the commission for access to information and other assistance.

RFA suggestions put forward by the public will be regarded as submissions to the exhibitions of the Commission's Background Reports parts C and D.

Participants who do not wish to make use of Commission's assistance may make a direct submission to the Background Reports.

Participants who wish to put forward views in forums rather than in formal submissions will have those views recorded and considered.

6.4.7 Forums

The Commission will convene forums for discussion. There will be an initial forum to discuss the participation process. There will also be forums to provide further information to participants and feedback on experience and progress as issues are identified and options are developed.

6.4.8 Time Frame

It is suggested that participants, if they so wish, form groups in September 1996 and familiarise themselves with background information available during September 1996 and October. It is expected that the information from the RFA studies will become available from mid October and be formally published as a part of Background Report early in November 1996.

During December 1996 to January 1997 the Tasmania-Commonwealth Joint Steering Committee will use public submissions in the further integration process. This stage of process will involve further consultation with those who put forward submissions on RFA integration.

6.4.9 Draft RFA Report

At the conclusion of the integration process the Steering Committee will draft RFA report. The Commission will publish this report in March 1997 for public comment. The exhibition period will include opportunities for discussion and feedback as well as formally inviting written submissions.

After consideration of the outcomes from this final round of public consultation the Tasmanian and Commonwealth Governments will finalise the RFA for Tasmania by 30 June 1997.

6.4.10 Public Feedback

Those who wish to use the assistance offered by the Commission should contact the Commission at the earliest opportunity. Others, however may make a direct submission to the Background Reports Parts C and D following publication of those documents in early November 1996.

Public feedback is invited on how participation in the integration process can be best achieved and public can be best involved.

Comments should be made to the Commission by 11 October 1996.

6.5 FORESTS AND FORESTRY INDUSTRY COUNCIL OF TASMANIA

6.5.1 Public Participation in Forest Management

The FFIC contains recommendations that Management Plans will be prepared for all State Forests with provision for proper public input.

The FFIC is preparing a proposal to Government on how this recommendation should be implemented.

There are already substantial opportunities provided by the Government for the public to participate in the forest planning process. These include :

- establishment by the forestry Commission of local community advisory groups to discuss specific local issues;
- issuing of draft management plans and policy option papers for public comment ; and
- discussion of proposals with affected landowners and user groups.

Public participation should occur throughout all stages of the planning process and can take many different forms.

The Strategy recommends that these opportunities should be developed into a consistent Statewide process.

There needs to ensure that the planning and decision making process is transparent; that all relevant information is available to all participants; that decisions are made in time; and that the plan has wide community support.

Some proposals under consideration for public participation in planning are :

* production of Management Plans for all State forest uses and values.
* formation of local community advisory groups to assist in the planning process.
* production of a separate resource document to provide a common data base for planning.
* public involvement in developing management options.
* draft management plans issued for public comment.
* an opportunity for final appeals.

No participants in the process can expect all their requirements to be met.

However, they can expect to be given every opportunity to put forward their views and to have them considered. Final decisions will still be made by Government and the Forestry Commission taking into account community opinions.

These proposals will lead to an improved decision making process with a significant degree of community involvement.

6.6 ECOLOGICALLY SUSTAINABLE DEVELOPMENT WORKING GROUPS : ECOLOGICALLY SUSTAINABLE FOREST USE–DRAFT REPORT

6.6.1 Preface

'The concept of ecologically sustainable development (ESD) has come to international prominence in the recent years as conservation and development issues have captured the attention of the public and world leaders. Although the idea has been around for some time, it was the release in 1987 of the Report of the World Commission on Environment and Development (WCED 1987) titled "Our Common Future (the so called Brundtland Report) which brought the issue into broad community focus. The Brundtland Report defined sustainable development as that which "meets the needs of the present without compromising the ability of future generations to meet their own needs". In doing so it erected international attention to the imperative of integrating environment and economic objectives to ensure sustainable development of economic and social systems.

In July 1989, Prime Minister of Australia issued a Statement on the Environment : Our Country Our Future. Following the release of the Statement, the Australian Government held a summit of industry, union and conservation organisations in order to commence an approach towards encouraging Australia's industry sectors and conservation group to embrace and apply the principles of ESD. A discussion paper outlining the concept of ESD in an Australian context was released for public comment in June 1990, as a first step in the process of developing a national ESD strategy.

Following the public comment phase, the Commonwealth established nine Working Groups to consider the implementation of ESD principles in sectors of Australia's economy which have significant inter-relationships with the environment. These were the agriculture, forest use, fishing, mining, energy production and use, manufacturing, tourism and transport sectors. Membership of the working Groups was drawn from industry, union, community groups, conservation organisations, CSIRO, ANZEC, and State and Commonwealth Governments.

The task of each Working Group was to identify the most important problem areas, set some priorities for achieving the changes desired, develop the solutions that meet both environmental and economic goals, and propose time frames for change that take account of Government's social justice policies and Australia's place in the world.

Public consultation is considered by the Government to be a vital part of the ESD process. The public consultation program is designated to provide information on issues to the Australian community, and feedback to the Working Groups'.

6.6.2 Forest Use Working Group–Executive Summary

6.6.2.1. 'Introduction....The draft conclusions and recommendations which follow, and which are presented more extensively in the report, are based on the following :

* the need to optimise *benefits to the community* from all forest uses, in order to improve material and non-material welfare and to intra and inter-generational equity objectives;' (pp. xii)

6.6.2.2. 'Draft Recommendation 13....that the States review their current land-use decision-making process with a view to ensuring that these processes

* recognise and consider all tangible forest values and potential uses and benefits;

* incorporate extensive *public consultation*;' (pp. xiv)

6.6.2.3. 'Forest Management–Objective....It is also essential that the *community* and the industry have an opportunity to be involved in the planning process, and ready access to the eventual operational decisions reached.' (pp. xiv)

6.6.2.4. 'Commercial Use–Objective....The Working Group has devoted its time to developing procedures and processes which it believes will ensure appropriate *economic returns to the community* from the commercial use of forests.' (pp. xxiii)

6.6.2.5. 'Draft Recommendation 25....If industry and community displacement does occur, appropriate programmes should be established to assist in relocation, redeployment, retraining and social adjustment based on community approach to assessing appropriate adjustment programmes including

* *community consultation;'* (pp. xxvii)

6.6.2.6. 'Draft Recommendation 32....That the strategic and operational forest management plans which are developed by forest management agencies responsible for conservation and economic uses based on the following principles

* all forest values and future benefits, including heritage values, being taken into account to access the most suitable management approach to optimise *benefits to the community;*
* full *public consultation;* (pp. xvii)

'6.6.3 Maintaining Biodiversity-Management of Reserves.... The management of reserves requires the development of conservation strategies and management plans. Ideally this process should include community consultation and involvement (particularly in the development of regional and local forest use management plans) to ensure that whole range of community values are taken into account.' (pp. 50)

'7.2. Optimising Economic Benefits to the Community within Ecological Constraints – Policies and Measures : Maximise community returns from use of public forests;

* *Maximising Community Returns* : As a publicly owned resource, the community has the right to expect that public forests provide the maximum returns to the community from all uses. Conceptually, capturing the economic rent inherent in the resource ensures the maximum return to the community from allocating property rights over public resources. Determining what constitutes the economic rent inherent in a resource is difficult, and developing policies to ensure it is received by the *community* within distorting market investment decisions is fraught with complexities.'

6.7 TASMANIAN PUBLIC LAND USE COMMISSION

6.7.1 Inquiry Into Tasmanian Crown Land Classifications

6.7.1.1. 'Department of Tourism Sport and Recreation

* Considered that the recommendations were a strong framework for rationalising the classification system and would ensure that Tasmania had a clearer and simpler system allowing for more effective management and greater community participation;
* recognised the special relationship between Aboriginal people and the land;' (6)

6.7.1.2. Local Government Association

* Commended the recommendations and the overall approach taken and said that the integrated and community based approach would be beneficial to the sound management of Crown land ;' (7)

6.7.1.3. 'Combined Environment Groups

* strongly endorsed community access to enforcement of management and planning;
* supported the conservation assessment of unallocated Crown lands but said that some areas should be allocated as wilderness or national parks immediately and that any assessments should take account of Aboriginal people's interests;'

6.7.1.4. 'Tasmanian Aboriginal Centre

Recommended that the Commission make it clear that it assumes the legitimacy of Crown ownership for the purposes of its inquiry but acknowledges the existence of the claim of Aboriginal people to those areas;

* raised various issues related to land rights and said that classification decisions can effectively disposes Aboriginal people;
* recommended that Aboriginal interests be considered before classifying any land in a way that would prejudice those interests;
* suggested that Aboriginal people should be exempted from adhering the prescribed management objectives so they can pursue cultural practices in reserves;
* said Aboriginal interests should be considered in all categories so that a separate category to protect Aboriginal interests was not necessary;
* should consider the question of compensation of Aboriginal people if rights to land are denied through classification;
* wished to be advised when unallocated Crown land is disposed of or sold;
* Flinders Island unallocated land should be returned to the Aboriginal community for management; and
* the concept of the Aboriginal Reserve category should be clarified and should not merely mean land administered by government.'

6.7.1.5. General Comments

* The motivation behind the IUCN classifications was government control of income at the expense of *local people* and a convenience for the future annexation of Australian land and World Bank.
* The new classification and management system had the potential to benefit conservation significantly and the possibility of *public input* to a Protected Lands Management Act be applauded.'

6.7.2 '3.0 The Protected Lands Classification System

6.7.2.1. Aboriginal Reserve

* an area of the land which contains sites, objects or places of significance to *Aboriginal people;* and
* which should be managed for the protection and maintenance of those sites, objects or places and / or use by *Aboriginal people.*

6.7.2.2. Public Reserve

* an area of Crown land which should be managed for a specific *community purpose.'*

6.7.3 '4.0. Planning and Management in the New System

6.7.3.1. Recommendations

* to encourage cooperative management programmes with Aboriginal people in areas of significance to them in a manner consistent with the reserve' purpose and other reserve's - purpose and other reserve management objectives;'

6.7.3.1.1. 'Sharing of management responsibility with the community – The commission has a statutory obligation, embodied in the objectives of Resource Management and Planning System, to promote the sharing of land management responsibility with the community. In view of this obligation and the keen local community interest in the management of Crown reserves, the Commission suggested that there should be some means whereby the community has access to a mechanism for seeking enforcement of management plans.'

6.7.3.1.2. Community participation in management – Submissions to the Inquiry Background Report alerted the Commission to the potential contribution of local communities to the management of locally important reserves. The Commission proposed that community interest and participation in reserve management could be achieved through the concept of Conservation Management Trusts established to manage locally important reserves. Within the framework of a Conservation Management Trust and an adopted management plan, specified community and interest groups could be empowered to manage certain reserves.

The majority of submissions welcomed the concept of trusts as a positive step towards greater community participation in land management. The main concerns of those rejecting the proposal were that development interests would be appointed and that natural resource management expertise would be lacking.

To ensure that Conservation Management Trusts would be community based and have members with appropriate natural resource management expertise, the Commission recommends that the types of community groups and levels of government from which membership should be drawn be prescribed in the legislation. The Commission also recommends that Trusts may be established only where there is an adopted management plan for the particular reserve(s).

The Commission believes that the concept of Conservation Management Trusts has a great deal of merit and, in certain circumstances, will play an important role in achieving community participation in the management of Crown land. Through representation on a trust, members of the community and other interest groups will be able to contribute actively to the management of reserve(s) associated with their establishment. Similar trusts established inter-state have worked well and given local communities a sense of ownership and responsibility for a reserve and a greater understanding and appreciation of the complexity of reserve management issues.

In keeping with the local community focus of the recommendation, the commission recommends that provisions for the establishment of Conservation Management Trusts apply to Cultural Landscapes, Conservation Areas and Nature Recreation Areas.'

6.7.3.2. 'Recommendation

It is recommended that :

6.7.3.2.1.

17. The Protected Lands Management Act :

- provide for the establishment of Conservation Management Trusts responsible for such Conservation Area, Cultural Landscape or Natural Recreation Area as may be described in the instrument of their establishment. Such a Trust to be established for a reserve(s) only where a management plan has been prepared and adopted;

  and
- provide for appointment, by the Minister, of members of a Trust, who are to include, where appropriate, nominees of :
  - Aboriginal groups;

6.7.3.2.2.

23. The Government of Tasmania consider the development of an

Aboriginal Crown land management policy with Aboriginal people with a view to inclusion of relevant arrangements in land management legislation; and
that the policy addresses the issues of :
joint management arrangements between government agencies and Aboriginal people for appropriate areas;

* managed access by specified Aboriginal people to natural resources traditionally exploited for food and / or cultural purposes.'

6.7.4 6.0 Control and Management of Protected Lands

'Management Plans

* Include in the functions of the Protected Lands Advisory Council a function to certify management plans for public exhibition and advise the minister on public representations to management plans.'

6.7.5 Public Land Use Commission Inquiry Process

* The details of the public consultation steps in the PLUC inquiry process have been presented in Fig. 6.2.

6.8 FORESTRY TASMANIA

6.8.1 Annual Report–1995-96: Forestry and the Tasmanian Economy

6.8.2 'Community Service Obligations

Forestry Tasmania is committed to ensure the efficient delivery of a wide range of *community services* including tourism and recreation facilities, education material and scientific research on non-commercial areas of State forest.

INQUIRY PROCESS

Government publishes Inquiry Terms of Reference for comment

Terms of Reference amended as necessary

Affected Agency Group Formed

Reference Panel Formed

Collection / collation of information on resources and uses of the land and background report prepared

Background Report published seeking public comment

Commission holds seminars, forums and or a public hearing

Assess submissions, collect additional data where relevant, prepare draft recommendations

Draft Recommendations published seeking public comment

Commission assesses public comment and prepares final recommendations

Final Recommendations to Minister and tabled before Both Houses of Parliament

Recommendations adopted, modified or rejected by Government

FOLLOWING AN INQUIRY

The implementation of the recommendations is a matter for the elected Government of the day subject to the will of Parliament. Implementation could be by administrative initiatives, action under existing land use legislature or legislative change.

Fig. 6.2 : Steps in PLUC Inquiry Process.

Objective 4 : Forestry Tasmania's objectives over the next four years are to :

* enjoy the broad support of the Tasmanian *community* for its management practices:

According to independent surveys on people's confidence in various employer groups, Forestry Tasmania rated highly in terms of credibility with the public. We aim to further improve this result. There have been increased offering programmes in State Forests. We are committed to the environment and to our customers and we always strive to improve the services to our shareholders. The Regional Forest Agreement, which is due to be completed by July 1997, will provide a framework which should bring renewed confidence in our forest and forest industry in the years ahead. There will be increased confidence for conservation outcomes as well as security in resources, which will result in confidence in the market place.

Forestry Tasmania looks forward to another year of steady growth and achievement against our objectives.

6.8.3 State of the Forests

A report to the Minister for Forests on the State of the Forests as on 30 June 1993

'Community Information and Consultation

4.1. *Public input into management plans for forested lands* : Both Parks and Wildlife Service and Forestry Commission Tasmania are required by law to seek public input into the preparation of management plans for public lands. Calls for public comment may be made at a number of stages during a plan's preparation, but it is often initiated when the first draft is released. Draft plans prepared under the Forestry Act 1920 have a mandatory public comment period of 60 days. A further comment period of a minimum of 30 days is required on plans submitted to the Minister for approval. Draft plans prepared under the National Parks and Wildlife Act 1970 must allow a public comment period of 30 days.'

6.9 TASMANIA'S FORESTS FOREST INDUSTRY STRATEGY

'*Recommendation 7* : Where private forest owners have private forest areas taken out of wood production for "community benefits" the beneficiaries should pay commercial rates of compensation to affected forest owners.'

6.10 FOREST MANAGEMENT PLAN–HUON FOREST DISTRICT

'2. *Management objectives* : The Forestry Act states that as a manager of forest land with a commitment to multiple use, the objectives of Forestry Tasmania are to optimise :

* the benefits to the public and the state of the non-wood values of forests.

  The specific management objectives for the plan Area are to:
* supply, as part of a sustainable yield unit of production forest, a range of wood products to forest industry and the **community;**'

'*Management prescriptions* : Interpretation will continue to encourage more thought and *involvement of the public* in planning how our forests will be managed in the future.'

6.11 TOURISM POLICY FOR TASMANIA'S STATE FORESTS

'*Forestry Tasmania and Tourism* : The amended Forestry Act 1994 states that Forestry Tasmania has following functions related to recreation :

* the provision to the public of information and education programs on sustainable forest management;
* the provision and maintenance of forest roads and other facilities for public access to and through State forest; and
* the provision and maintenance of recreation and public information facilities.'

'6.4. *Social and cultural sustainability* : Forestry Tasmania recognizes the potential of tourism to have adverse impacts on host communities. These impacts can include disruption of lifestyle, increases in local living costs, and the attachment of a commercial value to local culture. Therefore,

Forestry Tasmania will actively involve stakeholders to achieve social and cultural sustainability of tourism in State forests.

The promotion of social and cultural sustainability will be pursued through the following initiative :

* *involving local communities* and nature-based tourism industry networking.'

6.12 TASMANIA FIRE SERVICE

6.12.1 'Community Fireguard

Wildfire is an ever present threat in Tasmania. Whilst Tasmania does not have the same frequency of wildfire as Victoria, parts of Tasmania particularly the South East are nevertheless high risk areas. Living with the fact that wildfire may occur during every summer period is something we must come to terms with.

The last major fire disaster occurred on 7 February 1967 resulting in 62 deaths, the loss of 1400 structures, and thousands of animals. Since 1967 significant fires have occurred in 1973, 1982, 1988, 1991 and, more recently, history almost repeated itself on February 7, 1993.

Each year the Tasmania Fire service attends approximately 8000 fire calls and some 1500 of these are vegetation fires.

The Tasmanian Government strongly supports the work of the Tasmanian Fire Service in providing fire protection to the community at large. Volunteer and career members of the service will continue to give every effort but when wildfire occurs under adverse weather conditions it can be devastating and uncontrollable.

A large number of people now live in the bushland environment. Most people believe that Tasmania Fire Service firefighters will protect their homes during a bushfire. Generally this is true, however during a serious wildfire emergency there may not be enough fire fighting resources available to defend every home, so a great deal of responsibility rests with the home owner.

"Community Fireguard" is a program designed to allow people to help themselves by giving them the knowledge and understanding to be able to make informed decisions. It will give people the power to custom design strategies that meet the needs of each individual community.'

The detailed structure and process of Community Fireguard have been illustrated and laid out by the Government.

6.12.2 'Fire Management Area Committees

Fire Management Area Committees arise from sections 17, 18 and 20 of Fire Service Act 1979 as amended by Fire Service Reform Act 1995. They replace Local Fire Committees. Most parts of the State have been included in Fire Management Areas. Each Fire Management Area will have a Committee. This structure is intended to reduce the risk to the community from the fire.

Membership of fire Management Area Committees :

Mandatory representatives : The Chief of the Tasmanian Fire Service, usually the District Officer
Local Council(s) within the area
Forestry Tasmania (if Forestry Tasmania lands are in the area
Parks and Wildlife Service (if DELM lands are in the area)
Each Brigade Chief whose Brigade has responsibility for the area.

Discretionary representatives : Anyone the committee feels they need to include in order to get the job done.'

6.13 THE NATIONAL LANDCARE PROGRAMME

'....The administrative umbrella for the Landcare movement at a national level is the National Landcare Programme (NLP) within the Department of Primary Industries and Energy. The overall goal of the NLP is to achieve efficient, sustainable and equitable management of natural resources in Australia.

The NLP has three components :

* a community Landcare component established to assist community groups to work towards the sustainable management of land, water and vegetation resources in their local area;
* a commonwealth / state component where partnership agreements between the commonwealth and the states and territories provide a strategic framework for commonwealth funding of integrated projects within the states, emphasising institutional reform and planning; and
* a national component which funds commonwealth initiatives for integrated land and water management.'

7

Community Participation in Forest Management in India

'In agricultural countries like India and many of the colonies, forest set apart for village requirements are a matter of great importance in the rural economy of the country. The produce yielded includes fuel, poles, and withes for house building, wood for agricultural and domestic implements, fencing and thatching material, fodder, grass and other minor products, including edible fruits and plants which are particularly useful in time of famine. Under certain conditions regular grazing may be added to the benefits afforded by such forest, particularly in famine years.'

(Troupe, 1940)

The excerpts of different sections and laws emphasising community participation under various acts, policies and rules and regulations have been reproduced to understand the forestry framework of community participation in forest management in India.

7.1 INDIAN CONSTITUTION

'*Article 51 A (g) - Fundamental Duties* : "It shall be the duty of every citizen of India to protect and improve the unnatural environment *including forests*, lakes rivers and wildlife and to have the compassion for living creatures.'

7.2 INDIAN FOREST ACT 1927–CHAPTER III: OF VILLAGE FORESTS

'28. Formation of village - forests :

1. The State Government may assign to any village-community the rights of Government to or over any land which has been constituted a reserved forest, and may cancel such assignment. All forests so assigned shall be called village - forests.
2. The State Government may make rules for regulating the management of village-forests, prescribing the conditions under which the community to which any such assignment is made may be provided with timber or other forest-produce or pasture, and their duties for the protection and improvement of such forest.
3. All the provisions of this Act relating to reserved forest shall (so far as they are not inconsistent with the rules so made) apply to village-forests.'

7.3 NATIONAL FOREST POLICY 1988

'Objectives....(vi) Meeting the requirements of fuel - wood, minor forest produce and small timber for the rural and tribal population.

Recommendations....(iv) Minor forest produce provides sustenance to the tribal population, therefore, such produce should be protected, improved and their production be enhanced with due regards to generation of employment

(xi) The life of the tribals and other poor people living within or near the forests revolves round the forests. The rights and concessions enjoyed by them should be fully protected.

(xiii) The tribals should be closely associated in protection, regeneration and development of forests as well as to provide gainful employment to people living in and around the forests.

(xv) The grazing in the forest areas should be regulated with the involvement of the community. Special conservation areas, young plantation, regeneration areas should be fully protected.'

'Tribal and Forests....In order curb the encroachment, the forestry activities should be carried out by through Tribal Cooperative societies, labour cooperative societies, cooperative corporations, instead of the forest contractors.'

7.4 NATIONAL CONSERVATION STRATEGY AND POLICY STATEMENT OF ENVIRONMENT AND DEVELOPMENT 1992

'Action points include

–Increasing substantially the forest / tree cover in the country through massive afforestation and social forestry especially on all denuded, degraded and unproductive lands involving the local people;

–Meeting the rights and for requirements of fuelwood, fodder, minor forest produce and small timber of the rural and tribal population with due cognisance of the carrying capacity of forests;

–Afforestation on common lands by the local communities through usufruct - sharing schemes;

–Involvement of local people and dedicated grass roots non - governmental organisations in the afforestation programme and for protection of existing forest;'

7.5 WORLD BANK MADHYA PRADESH FORESTRY PROJECT 1995

The Madhya Pradesh Forestry Project financially aided by the World Bank (IDA) has become effective from 29th September 1995. The Project, with a total outlay of $ 300 million approximately, would be implemented in two phases of four and five years duration respectively.

The main beneficiaries of the project include forest fringe dwellers, a major proportion of whom are tribal people belonging to the poorest sections of the society. The Project incorporates specific measures to safeguard the interests of both landless and women, through participation in Village Forest Committees (VFCs), employment preference, and gender sensitive monitoring.

7.5.1 'Project Objective

To ensure participation of the people in management of forests and trees, taking special account of interests of tribal people and other disadvantaged groups.'

7.5.2 'The Strategy

The new strategy adopted by Madhya Pradesh Department (MPFD) involves changes in the sectoral policy framework. This would focus on creating a market oriented environment and an appropriate legislative and administrative framework for increasing participatory management of forest resource in which communities are treated as partners in the management of these resources.'

7.5.3 'Project Components

The Project has four main components:

7.5.3.1 Management Development : The strategy for the future development of the forestry sector in MP requires significant changes in sector management with thrust on :

* A change in approach and vision of MPFD for institutionalising participatory forest management;
* Development of new management systems to implement the new role of MPFD, based on support rather than command structures;
* Development of human resources and skills to enable staff to implement the new system.'

7.5.3.2 Forest Development : This is the largest component of the Project with approximately 60% of the outlay. The main objectives of this component are :

* the restoration of natural ecosystems and the preservation of biodiversity;
* reduction in land degradation;
* sustainable production; and
* improvement of natural regeneration through better forest floor management.

The strategy for forest development in degraded (Open) areas is slightly different from that for well stocked (Closed) forests. Community involvement in detailed planning and implementation of proposed forestry programmes has been adopted by MPFD as the cornerstone of the strategy in both areas. In closed forests, improved productivity would be achieved through natural regeneration and enrichment planting with a variety of species, including those of importance to local communities, and by adopting soil and moisture conservation measures.

In open forest areas, the species providing benefits to the communities would be given priorities. Here Joint Forest Management arrangements would be integrated with measures to provide alternative resources and income to reduce unsustainable exploitation of the forests. JFM has been defined as the sharing of products, responsibilities, control and decision making authority over forest land between forest department and local user groups, based on a formal agreement. This process of empowering the villages is in conformity with the process of decentralisation that has begun in the state with the introduction of Panchayati Raj. Participatory planning method have been adopted for forest management as well as village resource development. Efforts will be made, through JFM to increase the stake of the neighbouring communities in the management and utilisation of forest; and to create alternative sources of income and employment for villagers to reduce their dependence on the forest. JFM has already gained momentum in the state and currently around 4000 village level forest committees are in operation.

7.5.3.3 Two main types of forest development technologies to be adopted under the project would be :

* Assisted Natural Regeneration (ANR), and
* Rehabilitation of Degraded Forests (RDF).

Under ANR, promotion of natural forest regeneration, supported by enrichment planting, improved silvicultural practices, soil moisture conservation works and forest floor management works would be taken up over an area of about 16 million hectares.

It would include rejuvenation of flowered bamboo areas also.

In RDF, an area of about 74,000 ha would be managed by involving about 1140 villages under JFM. A unique Village Resource Development Programme (VRDP), based on participatory planning is to be implemented in these villages situated in forest fringe areas with an aim of generating alternative incomes or resources for villagers. These works are to be taken up by the village forest committees constituted within five kms periphery of the boundaries of the degraded forests and will be as per a microplan prepared through participatory rural appraisal (PRA).

Non-governmental organisations have an important role to play in implementing the VRDP component. Efforts would be made to associate committed voluntary agencies / NGOs with proven track records as interface between state forest department and the local village communities. Such organisations may prove well suited for motivating and organizing village communities for protection, afforestation and development of degraded forest land, specially in the vicinity of habitations. Such institutions would be encouraged to share their experience of gender specific planning with the communities and the forest department in formulating VRD plans.

The project would support VRDP through providing funds and promoting the process of institution building at the village level and within MPFD. Eco-development centres will be created in each participatory planning skills to field staffs.

7.5.3.4 Research and Extension : Forestry extension programmes focused on farms and community forestry would be supported in about 40 forest divisions through provision of extension material and equipment, farmer training and demonstrations. The private sector in MP, in context of the forestry sector, includes village communities, graziers, and farmers as well as forest based industries. The future role of the private sector will be to extend their involvement in farm forestry and agro-forestry. The livestock, which causes severe grazing pressure on the forests, are entirely controlled by private sector. Therefore the strategy to minimise grazing pressure on forest will depend to a great extent on the cooperation of owners in the form of increase in the production of cultivated fodder, and improvement of livestock productivity through breeding.

7.5.3.5 Biodiversity Conservation : Conservation of biodiversity would have three main thrusts :

* improved management and protection of protected areas (PAs) to increase their ecological viability and diversity;
* maintenance of ecological connectivity between protected areas and enhancement of PA network for the state;
* reduction in the dependency of communities on PA resource through sustainable management of forests in areas peripheral to the PAs, and through eco-development programmes for local populations.

These activities would be financed through establishment of an Eco-development Support Fund which would support implementation of village level, site specific microplans (Eco-development Plans) formulated through a participatory process.'

8. JOINT FOREST MANAGEMENT RESOLUTION OF GOVERNMENT OF MADHYA PRADESH, INDIA, FEBRUARY, 2000.

Many of the States in India have taken major decisions to decentralise the powers to the village level forest committees and empower them for the decision making for sharing mechanism and the management of the local forest resource. Attempts have been made to institutionalise the process through government orders and resolutions. Government of Madhya Pradesh in its latest resolution has made a breakthrough to strengthen the forest committees by explicitly defining their role and powers, and establishing linkages among various village level institutions. The contents of the resolution are as follows :

Subject : Amended resolution to obtain cooperation of people for protection and development of forests.

The National Forest Policy, 1988 envisages co-operation of the local people in conservation and development of forests. Accordingly, Ministry of Environment and Forests, Government of India issued instructions to all States on 1st June, 1990 that the tribals and other villagers living in or around forests will have the first right on the forest products. According to this principle, co-operation of the local public is being sought through the system of Joint Forest Management.

2. In view of the aforesaid principle laid down by the Government of India, the State Government has passed a resolution on 10th December 1991 to obtain people's co-operation in sensitive areas from the point of view of forest protection. The resolution also describes a detailed procedure for this purpose. In order to provide it a broad base and with the objective of obtaining of people's co-operation in all forest areas, the State Government issued an amended resolution on 4th January 1995.

3. According to the current practices of forest management

in the State, the forest areas of the State are divided into three parts (zones) :

First Zone : Forest areas included in the National Parks and Sanctuaries. These areas are extremely important from the viewpoint of bio-diversity conservation.

Second Zone : Other dense forest areas, which are used to obtain forest products under regular forestry works.

Third Zone : Those forest areas, which have become open due to biotic pressure, and need reforestation/restoration.

4. All the areas mentioned above have their own distinctive features. So with this background the State Government, while repealing the resolution of equal number, dated 4 January 1995, passes the revised resolution as follows:

4.1 Eco-development committees shall be constituted, for securing the co-operation of the people in the management of forests, in all the villages situated inside the National Parks and Sanctuaries, and in such villages outside the protected areas which are situated within five kilometers from the boundaries of these areas and which influence the protected area management, according to the principles of protected area management and in all the villages situated within a notified buffer zone of a protected area, where a buffer zone has been notified. Joint forest management committees already constituted in these areas will also be called as eco-development committees.

4.2 Forest Protection Committees shall be constituted in villages situated within five kilometers from the forest block boundaries in dense forests, except those covered under section 4.1.

4.3 Village Forest Committees shall be constituted in villages situated within five kilometers from the forest block boundaries of degraded forests, except those covered under sections 4.1 and 4.2.

5. Procedure for constituting Committees :

5.1 Meetings will be organised in the villages of the State, by the local forest staff, to apprise the people about the joint forest management, and thereafter, if the villagers voluntarily want to get involved in forest protection, development and management of forests, then on getting such information a formal meeting will be held in the village in the presence of a forest official, not below the rank of a forester, in co-operation with the local representatives of the people. An appropriate committee will be constituted, in accordance with the provision for the zone in which a village is situated, if 50% or more of the population of the village, which is eligible to vote, adopts a resolution, by a general majority, to this effect. In case both dense and degraded forests are situated near the village, then according to the predominance of the kind of forest area, the forest protection committee or the village forest committee shall be formed.

5.2 For the purpose of the constitution of committees, the habitations or groups of habitations or small villages or their groups, which include such communities which have been managing their affairs traditionally as a village, shall be treated as a village, in accordance with section 4 (B) of the Panchayat (Extension to Scheduled Areas) Act, 1996, irrespective of the fact whether that village is situated in a scheduled area (Schedule to the Constitution of India) or outside it. The committee shall be registered by the concerned Divisional Forest Officer (territorial) / Divisional Forest Officer (wildlife) / Director, National Park within one month of the adoption of the resolution, in accordance with section 4 of this resolution. All the villagers, who are eligible to vote, shall be the members of the general body of the committee. In the first meeting of the committee, which will be presided over by the Sarpanch of the respective village Panchayat, these members will elect the chairperson and the vice-chairperson, whose terms in office will be two years. Either of the chairperson or the vice-chairperson will necessarily be a woman.

5.3 If any forest committee already exists in the village, then that committee shall be recognised as a Joint Forest Management committee.

5.4 A federation of the chairpersons of the committees shall be constituted at the Forest Division level.

6. Executive:

Executive Committee consisting of minimum 11 and maximum 21 members (except the ex-officio members) shall be constituted as per the following guidelines: -

1. The committee shall nominate the Executive Committee by convening a meeting under the chairmanship of the elected Chairman of the concerned committee.

2. The Chairman / Vice-Chairman of the forest committee will also act as ex-officio Chairman / Vice-Chairman of the Executive Committee .

3. The Executive Committee shall also include members from schedule castes, schedule tribes and backward classes in proportion to their population in the Gram Sabha of the village, as far as possible.

4. Minimum 33 per cent members of the Executive Committee will be women, in which one representative from each women Self Help Group, if working in the village, will be compulsorily selected.

5. Minimum of 2 members (1 male and 1 female) from landless families, if available will be included in the Executive Committee, out of which, one representative should compulsorily be elected from the Self Help Group working in the village.

6. All Panch / Sarpanch residing in the village will be ex-officio members of the committee.

7. If Rajiv Gandhi Watershed Mission Committee is working in the village then one beneficiary from each beneficiary group will be member of the Executive Committee.

8. For rest of the members of the Executive Committee, it will be essential to nominate one representative from each of the user groups of village resources created in the village, if available.

9. Besides the above members, the Beat Guard or Forester in-charge of the concerned forest area will be ex-officio Secretary of the Executive Committee.

10. Except the ex-officio members, the term of the other members of the Executive Committee will be for a period of 2 years.

7. Selection of Area :

7.1 After the constitution of the committee, forest area for different kinds of committees will be selected by the Divisional Forest Officer (territorial)/Divisional Forest Officer (wildlife)/ Director, National Park shall, in consultation with the executive committee. An officer, not below the rank of a range officer, can be authorised by the above mentioned forest officer, for this purpose. For the selection of forest area for the committee, consideration will be given to the distance between the forest and the village and the area traditionally used by the villagers for Nistar purposes. The area will be selected on the basis of the recommendation of an officer of the rank of Assistant Conservator of Forests regarding its technical suitability. In case of a difference of opinion related to the selection of an area, the decision of the concerned Divisional Forest Officer (territorial)/Divisional Forest Officer (wildlife)/Director, National Park shall be final.

7.2. No forest area shall be selected for the eco-development committees constituted inside the protected areas. Only for the eco-development committees constituted in the villages situated outside the protected areas, which influence the management of the protected area, forest area outside the protected area can be selected under provision of section 7.1.

8. Microplan

8.1 After the constitution of the committee, as soon as possible, a microplan shall be prepared by the villagers, with the participation of the Forest Department. The microplan shall cover both the area of the village as well as the forest area selected for the committee. The microplan shall include provisions for both forest management as well as village resource development programme. The microplan shall propose works/activities on the basis of the estimated availability of resources. Other works shall be included in a separate annexure, on the basis of priority. The name of the executing agency and the possible source of funding shall also be shown with the works. The microplan shall be submitted to the district level forest officer by the committee for approval. The microplan shall be approved after examining its technical and legal aspects.

8.2 The principles of forest/wildlife management are prescribed in the existing working plan/management plan. The works proposed in the area selected for the committee shall be in accordance with these principles. The microplan shall ensure that the laws/rules applicable to forest/wildlife management are not violated.

8.3 The State Government shall arrange for the funds required for executing the forest works included in the plan. In addition, the committee and the Forest Department shall also arrange for funds for works, which can reduce the dependence of the villagers on forests, through the DRDA, other departments, Panchayats and other sources. For the execution of these works, a contribution of 25% from the committee members, in the form of labour, shall be necessary, as far as possible. An amount equivalent to the labour contributed shall be remitted in the account of the committee for use in the village resource development works.

8.4 The microplan shall be prepared by the Forest Department and the committee, in collaboration with other development departments. Technical and financial resources, for the execution of the village development works included in the microplan, can be obtained from other develop departments of the State.

8.5 The economic development activities, which are ecologically sound and sustainable, shall be included in the microplan on priority basis.

8.6 For the co-ordination of the activities to be executed through the microplan, in each district, a co-ordination committee, under the chairmanship of the chairperson of the permanent forest committee of the district Panchayat, shall be constituted by the

State Government. This committee will convene a meeting at least once in four months for affecting co-ordination. The Janpad Panchayat Chairperson and the district level officers of all the concerned departments shall be the members of this committee. One district level forest officer, nominated by the Conservator of Forests, shall be the member-secretary of the committee.

9. Meetings

Meeting will be convened by the Secretary with the consent of the Chairperson. It will be compulsory to convene at least one meeting in three months. Normally the meetings will be presided over by the Chair person/Deputy Chairperson, but in his/her absence members may choose one of the members as Chairperson for the meeting. The General Body Meeting will be convened at least once in six months. The time and place of the meeting will be decided in consultation with the Chairperson. The proceedings of the meeting will be recorded in a register maintained for this purpose. The forthcoming executive body will be elected in the last meeting of the General Body in the year of the expiry of the term of the executive body. It will be compulsory to convene this meeting one month before the expiry of the term of the executive body.

10. Quorum

For the executive body, 50% of the members and for the General Body, 30% members will be essential to fulfil the quorum.

11. Rights and Duties of the Committee

11.1 Rights

The Committees will derive following benefits subject to the satisfaction of the District level Forest Officer that the committee has satisfactorily performed the works pertaining to Joint Forest Management.

1. All families of the Committees would be entitled to royalty free Nistar, every year, subject to availability, taking only harvesting expenditure.

2. All forest committees would be given from time to time cent per cent share of the produce obtained from the thinning of timber coupes and clearing of culms in degraded bamboo forests executed on the basis of provisions of the Microplan/Working Plan.

3. In the forest area allotted to the Forest Protection Committee, out of the forest produce obtained from final fellings of bamboo/timber coupes, based on the provisions of the Working Plan, forest produce, equivalent to the value of the 10% of produce after deducting the corresponding harvesting costs, would be made available to the committee. Calculation of the price would be made on the basis of the sanctioned Malik Makbooja timber/bamboo rates of the concerned circle.

4. In the open/degraded forest area allotted to the Village Forest Committee, out of the forest produce obtained from the plantation/rehabilitation of degraded forests/pasture development works done in the area/final felling of the planted area, 30% of the value of the produce, after deducting the corresponding harvesting costs, would be made available to the committee. Calculation of the price would be made on the basis of the sanctioned Malik Makbooja timber/bamboo rates of the concerned circle.

5. For Eco-Development Committees which are situated within the Protected Areas, where felling is banned, value of the forest produce will be given to such committees. The price of the produce would be equivalent to the price of the produce made available to the Forest Protection Committee working in the area adjoining to the concerned Protected Area. This arrangement would be in addition to the annual Nistar facilities received by the Committees. The Eco-development Committees situated outside the Protected Areas will derive benefits as mentioned above depending upon the density of the forests allotted to them. Out of the amount received by the committee from the final felling, 50% would

be distributed to the members of the committee in cash, 30% would be spent for village resource development and 20% would be spent on forest development.

6. Rights of the committee with reference to minor forest produce would be in accordance with the decision of the Government of Madhya Pradesh taken from time to time under the provisions of the Panchayat (Extension to Scheduled Areas) Act, 1996.

7. In case a committee co-operates in the apprehension of an offender in forest offence case registered in the area of the committee, fifty percent of the amount of the compensation/fine recovered from offenders, after compounding of the case or after a decision by the court, shall be deposited in the account of the committee, which will be used for the development of the village resources.

8. If a member of the committee does not co-operate with the committee in the activities of the committee, does not abide by the decisions of the committee or commits a forest offence, the committee, through a decision in the general body meeting, may deprive him/her of his/her eligibility for obtaining Nistar and may terminate his/her membership. But before taking this action, the member will be given an opportunity to present his/her case. The action taken in connection with the forest offence will be in addition to this action.

9. The committee shall be able to transfer all or specific powers to the executive through a resolution in the general body meeting.

11.2 Duties

1. The committee shall elect the Executive body.

2. The committee members shall protect forests from fire, illegal grazing, illicit felling, illegal transportation, illegal mining, encroachments and poaching and render all co-operation to the Forest Department in these. To achieve this objective the committee, with the help of its members, will take necessary steps for the protection of forests.

3. Information regarding person/persons causing damage to forests and wildlife or indulging in illegal entry/unauthorised activities in the forest, will be given to the Forest Department.

4. If any wildlife accidentally strays out of the forest area then ensuring its protection, information will be given to the nearest forest officer.

5. The committee will prepare a Micro-management Plan and Annual Work Plan in participation with the Forest Department. The plans will incorporate community, beneficiary oriented, necessity based and site specific programmes. Activities directly or indirectly related to forest and wildlife protection will be given priority. Micro-management Plan will be signed by the Forest Range Officer on behalf of the Forest Department and Chairman of the Executive Committee on behalf of the committee. Based on Micro-management Plan an Annual Work Plan will be prepared for every financial year. For the implementation of the Annual Work Plan an advance of the amount upto 10 per cent can be given at a time to the committee. Implementation of sanctioned plans will be done by the committee. If any committee is not performing the work satisfactorily or not interested in carrying out the works then in such case the work will be carried out by the Department.

6. The committee members, on being informed of any forest offence within their area or outside their forest area shall report immediately the same to the concerned Beat Guard/Game Guard. At the same time, the committee members shall also assist the Forest Department in apprehending the culprits involved in forest offence. The apprehended culprits and seized forest produce will be handed over to the concerned forest officer.

7. The Memorandum of Understanding will be signed between the Chairman of the Committee and District level forest officer or an officer authorised by him/her.

8. As per the Para 8.3 of the Resolution, in the implementation of the Micro-management Plan, the contribution of the committee members in form of labour component will be ensured as far as possible.

9. During inquiry of the forest offence the committee members

will assist the staff of the forest department.

10. The Committee would maintain account of funds received from different sources and the expenditure would be audited by the agency appointed by the Forest Officer.

11. The list of the members would be maintained in a register by the Committee. Apart from this the Committee would maintain other registers and records specified by the Forest Officer.

12. In the context of Forest Protection, the members of the Committee would be treated as Public Servant similar to Foresters under different acts during patrolling of forests and they will be provided legal protection like Public Servants for the works done *bona fide* in the interest of the Government. In the event of injury or death, during efforts made to stop or prevent the forest offences, the compensation similar to forest staff would be provided.

13. An amount equivalent to 50% of the compounding amount or compensation/fine decided by the Court to be recovered from the offender would be deposited in the committee's account if the committee takes cognizance of the forest offence and helps in apprehending the forest offender within the jurisdiction of their area.

12. Powers and Duties of Forest Officer :

The powers and duties of the District level Forest Officer would be as under. If nothing is specified in this resolution the said officer can devolve this power to an officer of the rank not inferior to Range Officer.

12.1 Powers

1. Allotment area for the committees as per provision under section 7.1.

2. Approval of the Micro management plan.

3. Scrutiny of committee's accounts and rules made for distribution of forest produce and sharing of benefits among members.

4. If the committee does not discharge its duty envisaged under section 11.2 and corrective measures are not taken even after the written communication by the Forest Officer to the committee, the Forest Officer may dissolve the committee and terminate Memorandum of Understanding. In this situation the entitlement of members of the committee to receive benefits provided in section 11.1 would cease.

12.2 Duties

1. Organise meeting at village level for the constitution of the committee as per section 5.1.

2. Registration of the committee.

3. Observe election of committee and Executive Committee.

4. Provide training and technical help to the committee members in preparation and implementation of the Microplan.

5. Provide financial resources according to section 8.3 for works included in the Microplan and establish co-ordination with other departments for works mentioned in section 8.4.

6. Assist committee in discharging its duties and monitoring and helping them in resolving internal disputes.

7. Monitoring and evaluation of works executive by the committee.

8. Appoint agency for the annual audit of committee's account and getting account examined through them.

9. Provide forest produce and other benefits from the area allotted to committee as per the provision of sub sections 1 to 3 of section 11.1.

10. Ensure appropriate participation of weaker sections of the committee especially women in committee's decision and benefit sharing.

13. Appeal

1. The concerned person would be eligible to file an appeal against order passed against him under sub section 8 of section

11.1 within one month from the date of order to the Range Officer of that area.

2. Appeal can be made against the order of the Forest Officer to dissolve committee within one month from the date of order to the Federation constituted under section 5.4

3. The decision of the above appellate officers would be final.

(NOTE : The original resolution in Hindi has been translated into English)

8

Community Participation in Forest Policies of Some Other Countries

8.1 The salient points pertaining to community participation in the forest policies of some other countries have been quoted below. Although some of the policies referred to are not the latest ones but still these give an idea about the approach and vision of the policies towards community participation and forest management in these countries.

8.1.1 China

Manage forests according to a multi-use sustained yield principle to maximise social benefits in times of watershed protections and timber production.

Regardless of ownership, public interest should be paramount and dominant value of forest management is protection.

Production forests are maintained from an economic standpoint.

Permanent ownership of natural forests rest with government.

8.1.2 Fiji

Protect and develop natural forests/vegetation.
To develop production.
To ensure best use of timber species.
To establish and promote and export trade in timber.
To check soil erosion and cover eroded areas.
Land owner participation-growing interests among them.
No active participation.

8.1.3 Indonesia

Increasing the productivity of the forests.
Forest protection.
Policies for land use.

8.1.4 Malaysia

Promote effective participation by rural people in the forests and wood based industries consistent with government policies.

8.1.5 Nepal

The national forest plan, 1976 recognizes the legitimate basic forest product needs of the local people.

In accordance with this plan, the Panchayat forest and Panchayat protected forests rules were promulgated in 1978.

The intention was to handover parts of the government forest for management to local communities.

This was further reinforced with the promulgation of the decentralisation act 1982.

Recently, lease whole forest rules entitle Nepalese citizens to have 18 hectares in the Tarai and 4 hectares in the hills to plant trees for firewood, and medicinal plants on payment of nominal fee of rupees 15 per hectare to the government.

Forest Act 2049 (1993) of Nepal defines "Community Forest" as - 'A National Forest handed over to an users' group pursuant to Section 25 for its development, conservation and utilization for the collective interest. Chapter 5 (Sections 25-30) of the Act deals with the provisions relating to the regulations for the handing over, control and management of the community forests.

8.1.6 Pakistan

The National Conservation Strategy 1995 recommends for afforestation on marginal private lands by land owners and community forestry, but does not mention about direct community participation in the forest management.

8.1.7 Philippines

No thrust for community participation in forest management. Indifference of general public to forestry.

8.1.8 Thailand

To organise forests and forest margin populations to use appropriate agricultural technology.

Social forestry to reduce dependence of people on forests.

Forest village programme of Royal Forest Department: a location of 2-4 hectares of land to participatory households and encouragement of voluntary participation.

8.2 NEED OF CHANGES IN FOREST POLICIES

The following issues have been identified in the different forest policies of the developing countries (Asian Productivity Organisation 1976).

8.2.1 India

Need to modify policies pertaining to grazing, rights and concessions for forest dependent people, encouragement and support to private and commercial growers, social forestry, legislation pertaining to restriction on harvesting and marketing of forest products.

8.2.2 Nepal

Inconsistency between forestry legislation and decentralisation act, absence of updated forest maps.

8.2.3 China

Conflicts of land use between forests and park management agencies.

8.2.4 Korea

Constraints imposed by various agencies responsible for forestry and park and recreation.

8.2.5 Hong Kong

Agriculture and Fishery Department is responsible for forestry and park management.

8.2.6 Thailand

Need for revision of forestry legislation to facilitate co-ordination between public and private sector.

8.2.7 Fiji

Revision for better co-ordination of the government and semi-government organisations having roles to play in forest management.

8.2.8 Malaysia

National Forestry act and National Forest policies exist but states not compelled to adopt. National Forestry council is only a forum and its decisions are left to states - may or may not implement. Forest resources are utilised for other non-forestry activities.

8.3. General

Security of tenure is a universal problem in forestry in developing countries. Climate, natural disasters, environmental and ecological constraints are the important factors for which environment impact assessment need to be carried out. Also, the forestry activities need to be integrated with other developmental activities.

9

Discussion

The review of the forest policies of different countries and international organisations including FAO and World Bank and the recommendations of Agenda 21 categorically indicate that community participation is an essential ingredient for the sustainability of natural resources including forests.

The forest policies are mainly about the people and it is a common pitfall to think only of the forest resource while developing forest policy. It is the people who have to make the policy work who are intended to benefit from it. In order to institutionalise the concept and mechanism of community participation for sustainable forest management, it is imperative that necessary institutional changes are incorporated in the forest policies to empower and strengthen the community organisation. For this, modifications and reforms in the rules and regulations and laws which stem from the forest policies need also to be made.

The World Forestry Congress and other international organisations including FAO emphasise upon the management of every hectare of forest to the best advantage and in the best interests of all people. While analysing the broad descriptive features of the forest policies of different countries of the world, FAO has pointed out as one of the features being the distinction between types of ownership, a particularly important aspect from the policy point of view; the broad categories are publicly and privately owned forest land, but further sub-division, e.g. publicly owned into state owned and other categories are also important.

9.1 TOWARDS THE NEW APPROACH OF FOREST POLICIES

It is apparent from the analysis of the different forest policies that during the last one decade there has been a shift over from revenue oriented forest management to conservation and from conservation to the community based forestry management.

In most of the developing countries, there has been a long tradition of forest management and over the last two decades, consequent to the phenomenal increase in the biotic pressure as a result of escalation in the population of both human and livestock, usufructs emanating from the forest policies have been oriented towards the benefits and sharing of the forest dependent communities. Now the forest policies tend to pay attention to the needs of rural people for fuel and other domestic purposes. The forest policies are switching over to the need for participation of the people for the management of forests. The main trends of the forest policies in the developing countries include:

* replacement of uncontrolled exploitation, selected areas with conservation forest management;
* more plantations and community and social forestry;
* sharing of benefits with the forest dependent communities;
* involving communities and the management of forests; and
* encouraging communities to participate to some extent in decision making.

In the developed countries, the situation is a little different because the communities are not directly dependent on the forest resources. The main thrust of wood production policies in most developed countries with limited forest resources has been to raise production quickly and economically by plantation forestry. Community participation has been adopted as a part of the forest policies in many of the developed countries but since the communities are not directly dependent on the forests, the actual participation is quite limited only by those who are directly affected by the policies or the activities.

9.2 COMMUNITY INVOLVEMENT IN DECISION MAKING

Involvement of the community in the decisions which concern their future regarding the management of forests is a pre-requisite. Lower participation is often a sign of authoritarian situation one in which a person or a group imposes his/their ideas on individuals or the community. Decisions thus come from those in authority, rather than being made by the people who will carry out the work in the future.

Where decision are made by voting or consultation with all the people concerned free to express themselves, and decision are finally stated by an elected group the decision making process is considered to be participatory. More often decisions made by committees are somewhat short of full participation but not absolutely authoritarian. A distinct advantage of authoritarian approach to decision making is that action is usually taken right away, which gives a sense of action and accomplishment.

The situation is different when people sit down and decide amongst themselves to do something in their own way, not just to please someone else. If women are involved in decision which are crucial to their lives there can usually be a fair amount of confidence that something lasting will take place. If there is substantial agreement, preferably a consensus of all concerned, it is possible to feel more confident about how long the forest resources will last. The way a decision is made has a direct influence on how well it will be carried out: this is called the process of decision making. It is the means to the results. It is a necessary step before people take on the tasks they will have to perform to bring about the desired results. The need for the participatory process in decision making needs to be stressed in order to achieve lasting results. The objectives of the resource management should match with people's requirements, interests, thinking and vision.

The quality of the participation is essentially critical to how the programme is in the long run. Participation may be by a small group of people who represent only themselves and no more than a group of opportunists.

9.3 INVOLVEMENT OF NON-GOVERNMENT ORGANISATIONS

To develop the capacity to utilise forests in effective land-use systems, planning must take place within the community. The lack of local community organisations has been found to be a key barrier to forest management and rural development. For successful sustainable forest management, a forestry must establish a partnership with organised community groups. A high degree of community organisations can be observed in countries where forestry has become an integral part of rural development programmes.

In many countries, non-governmental community organisations have been found to play an important role in effective forest management. Some of the following examples illustrate the growing significant role of non-governmental organisations in the forest management:

China

Agricultural communes have participated in massive forestry programmes.

Korea

Reforestation through a system of 21,000 village forestry associations, regional forestry associations, unions, national federation of forestry association.

Japan

Half of forest land owned by small holders with less than 5 hectares; village forest owners association organised to carry out several activities aimed at rationalisation of forest management and increased forest productivity.

Sweden

Forest owners association played an important role in the improvement of forest utilisation and quality on small forest plots.

These examples indicate that community organisations which co-ordinate the forestry activities have been successful in countries while the ownership of forests is collective in private hands. Traditionally reaching a consensus and co-ordinating giant activities in the rural community was accomplished through multi-functional organisations which could integrate new tasks into village activities.

In many countries these traditional organisations have been replaced by a formal administration which may still co-ordinate all village activities and therefore must be utilised when starting forestry activities.

In the absence of community organisations in forest management popular movements sprang up motivated by economic needs. Chipko (tree-huggers) phenomenon, a Gandhian Movement started in UP (India) in 1973 by community members who clung to trees in order to save these trees from felling by contractors is one example. The Chipko Movement went to gain a large following specially among village women.

Other popular people's movements against environmental degradation include:

- Puket's Movement in Thailand 1986
- Bataan's Movement in Philippines
- CHICO (Bonito) Movement in Philippines
- Friends of the Earth Movement in Malaysia
- Bucket Merry Movement in Bakun Sarawak

Popular movements can generate such enthusiasm and mobilise voluntary labour. NGOs can promote forest management goals by channelising the power to constructive directions. An extension organisation can also seek partnership with organisations and groups that work for spiritual and material improvement of rural communities. Religious organisations, environmental groups and international aid organisations, missions, youth groups, women's organisations, political organisations, etc. can play an effective role to facilitate and strengthen the role of communities in management of natural resources including forests. Voluntary organisations, often idealistic groups can lend moral support to forest management programmes both at national and local levels. They can act as useful channels for transmitting information to villages and provide logistic and financial support.

Because of a lack of education, training and literacy at village level, specially in the developing countries, the non-governmental organisations can play a vital role in mobilising and motivating the communities for sustainable development and can act as an effective link between the people and the governmental organisation.

9.4 FROM PASSIVE PARTICIPATION TO ACTIVE INVOLVEMENT

Although most of the policies recommend and envisage for community participation in the management of forest resources and also recommends for the participation in decision making but the lack of corresponding changes in the legislation and administrative framework does not ensure the active involvement of the communities in the decision making and the management of forests.

In order to ensure the active involvement of the communities, people have to be empowered and strengthened and a system of community control needs to be evolved (Figure 9.1).

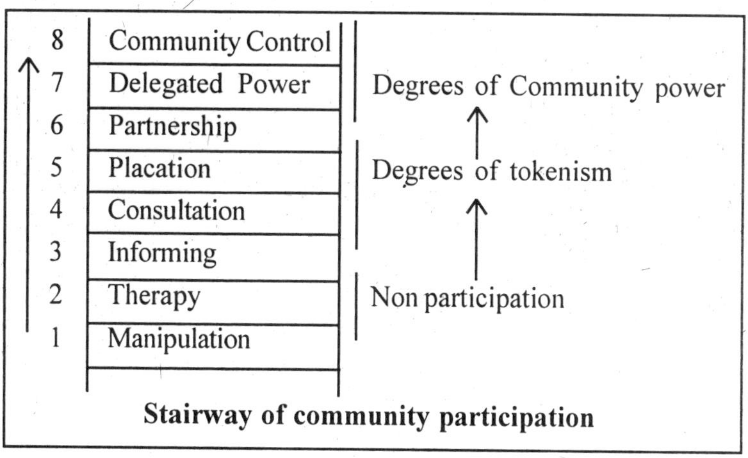

Fig. 9.1 : Degree of Community Participation

People have to be involved at all levels and there has to be a proper sharing of not only the benefits but the sharing of responsibility and accountability have also to be ensured. The people at the grass-root level have to be empowered and their confidence has to be strengthened. The sharing of power and encouraging leadership are also necessary in order to institutionalise the community participation as a system (Figure 9.2).

Community Participation for Sustainable Forest Management – Levels and Extent of Participation

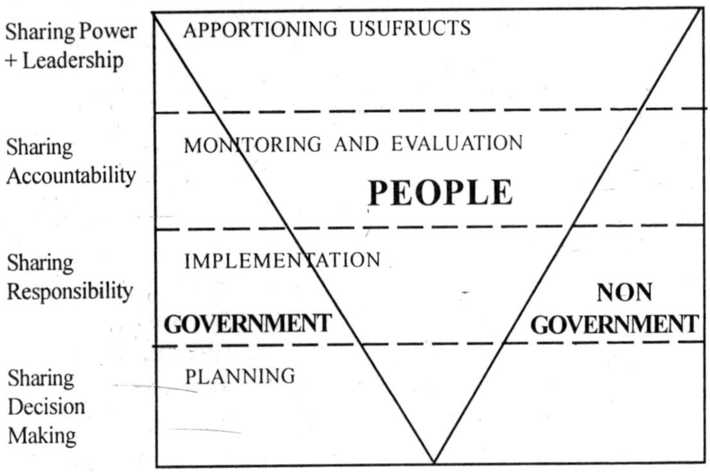

Fig. 9.2 : Levels and Extent of Community Participation

9.5 ECOSYSTEMS APPROACH

In order to manage the forests in a sustainable manner and link it with the sustainable development of the people, there is a need to adopt the ecosystems approach for the sustainable forest management and the sustainable development.

Since people are directly dependent on the forest not only for their livelihood but also intimately integrated culturally and ecologically, therefore, people form a part of the ecosystem and

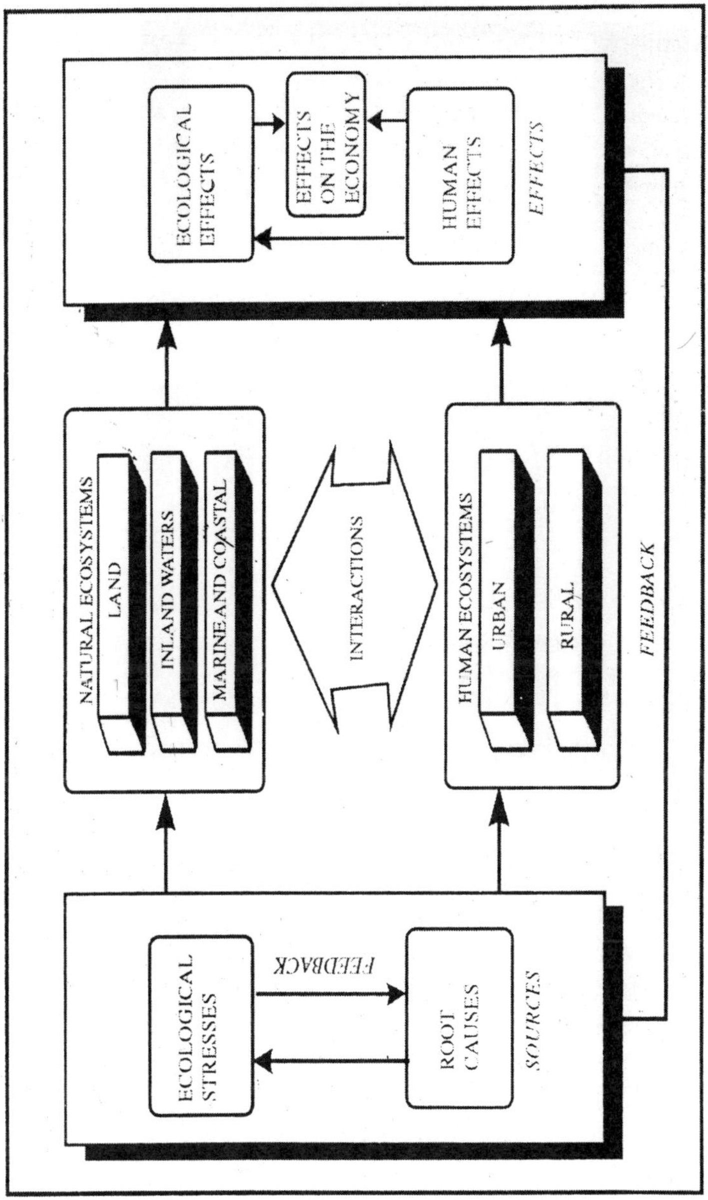

Fig. 9.3 : Ecosystem Approach Framework

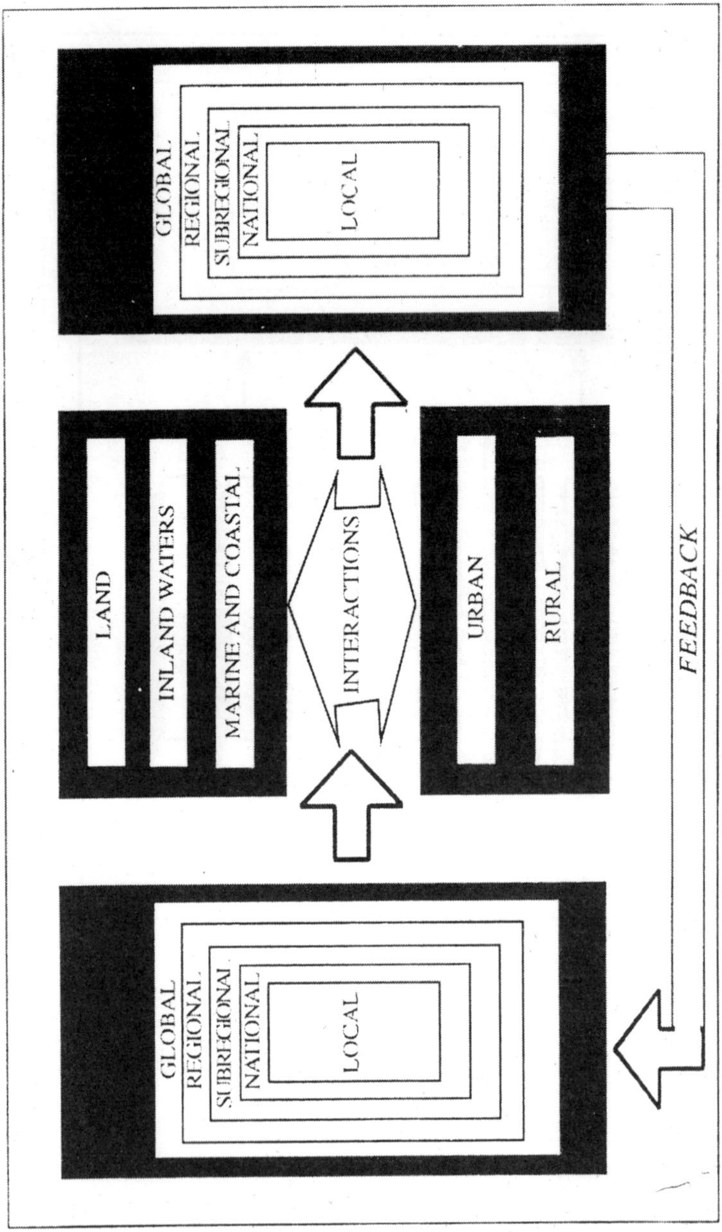

Fig. 9.4 : Framework of Various Functional Levels

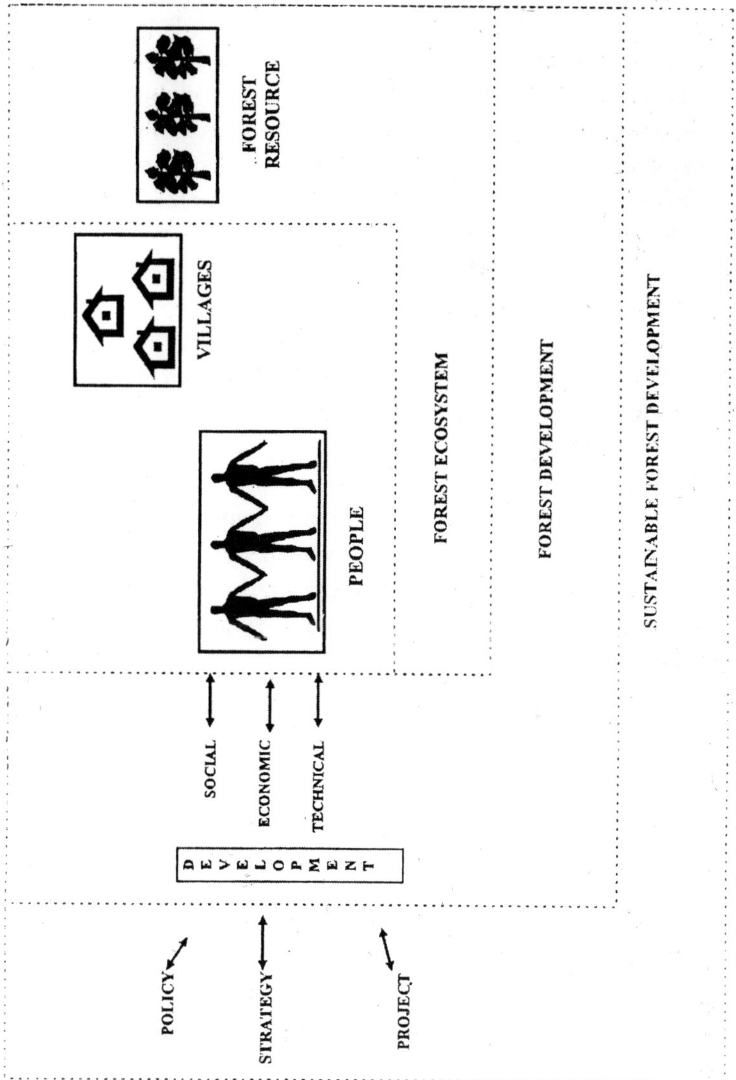

Fig. 9.5 : Holistic Ecosystem Approach for Sustainable Forest Management

while deciding management issues and taking policy decisions, people have to be considered as an integral component of the ecosystem (Figure 9.3), and they have to be involved at various levels of administration and management (Figure 9.4).

As all policies, strategies and projects are ultimately oriented towards the social economic and technical development of the people, therefore, people should be considered as an integral part of the system for the sustainable development. A holistic ecosystem approach needs to be adopted and implemented for the sustainable forest development (Figure 9.5).

9.6 RESEARCH NEEDS

In order to institutionalise the community participation mechanisms in actual practise in forestry management there is a scope of intensive research to:

* critically examine the existing models of community involvement and evaluate their strengths and weaknesses.
* identify and establish verifiable and well defined indicators of community participation for sustainable forest development.
* improvise existing models and/or develop new workable practical models for community involvement for sustainable forest management.
* develop an appropriate package for training and education for community participation in sustainable forest management at all levels.

10

Epilogue

* Most of the countries and international organisations have recognised community involvement as an essential tool for the sustainability of the forest resources. The forest policies, acts and other forestry related documents enacted by these countries and the recommendations of the forestry linked organisations clearly endorse and manifest the recent chan in attitude and approach in the forest management.

* The United Nations Food and Agriculture Organisation has not only strongly advocated for the people oriented forest management system but also recommended that the forest policies of all the countries should ensure the participations of communities at all levels, specially in decision making, implementation of activities and sharing of benefits. Other international organisations viz. UNEP, UNIDO, World Bank have also corroborated the concept of community participation.

* The Rio Earth Summit and Agenda 21 recommendations not only advocate for the necessity of the community involvement for Sustainable Forest Management but also for the other forestry related functions and environmental issues. Changes in administrative, legal and technical, and also political frameworks have also been recommended to facilitate the community involvement for sustainable forest management.

* In Australia, public participation has been accepted as an integral

part of the strategy of forest management. Public are involved in the formulation of new policies, acts and programmes related to forestry through discussion in seminars and submissions. Their involvement in the implementation of the policies and programmes and incentives need to be addressed. The involvement of communities is voluntary and the discussion with various officers of the different Tasmanian Government Departments including Land Management, Environment, Forestry etc. indicates that the actual participation in the form of submissions is about fourteen per cent with respect to the total population.

* The community participation in the forest management in India has gained a significant priority in the National Forest Policy of 1988.

* The policy clearly defines the provisions for participation of communities in decision making, sharing of benefits and incentives. The protection of forests by local village forest protection committees has been linked with the sharing of usufructs desired as a result of the protections. The mechanism of participation has been defined but in order to institutionalise the concept of community participation, the necessary changes in the other associated policies related to property and traditional rights need to be ensured.

* Although there is a global change in the trend in the forest management from top-bottom approach to bottom-top approach and all forest policies envisage community participation, nevertheless the actual implementation of the whole concept yet requires serious consideration. It may be required to evolve a system where the community participation becomes self regulatory and the government and non-governmental organisations may act as facilitators, to strengthen the communities for their sustainable development which stems from the sustainable management of the forest resource.

* In order to instutionalise the mechanism of community participation, it may be required to empower the people and strengthen their confidence to channelise their inherent traditional knowledge. To achieve this goal a strategy may be evolved to bring about necessary changes in the administrative, legal and political frameworks.

* For effective community participation in sustainable forest management and sutainable community development, a holistic integrated ecosystem approach needs to be adopted, and the forest dependent people have to be considered as an integral component of the ecosystem.

* All the forest policies and acts may be reviewed from time to time to make them more suitable to the requirements and vision of the community people, and in this process the communities may be directly involved at all levels. Further intensive research work may be undertaken to critically analyse the policies and acts and evolve workable self regulatory models for community participation in sustainable forest management and the SUSTAINABLE COMMUNITY DEVELOPMENT.

11

Recommendations

- * The forest policies, acts and other forestry related documents may be reviewed in the light of necessity of changes required in the structure, administrative, legislative and economic framework to match the requirements and vision of the communities and ensure the 'self regulated participatory system of forest management.'

- * The forestry linked policies and acts should clearly spell out

  - – the rights and concessions of the communities on the forest resource;
  - – the reponsibilities and accountabilities of the communities in the management system;
  - – traditional rights and ownership of land and sharing of usufructs and forest products;
  - – mechanisms to ensure implementation and enactment of the community involvement laws; and
  - – the roles of various components viz. people, government and non-governmental organisations and their responsibilities and accountabilities.

- * All the future forestry related projects and schemes need to include community involvement as an essential component and the communities may be involved at all levels from the beginning of the formulations.

* There appears a dire need to integrate the forestry activities and management with other activities like agriculture, horticulture, tourism, fisheries and rural development programmes which have direct and indirect impacts on the communities and ultimately on forest resources. Thus it requires an integrated holistic approach to the whole process.

* In developing countries, the forest management requires to be linked with the economy of the forest dependent people with provision for alternative income along with intensive educations, training and research for development of skills; whereas in developed countries the communities may be more intimately and directly involved with education, training and project formulation.

* The policies and acts may be required to strengthen the traditional knowledge and confidence of the communities. An attempt should be made to

  – facilitate the channelisation of the indigenous knowledge by creating a congenial atmosphere for this education and training;
  – use the indigenous knowledge in improvising the indigenous technologies for effective resource management;
  – document the indigenous traditional and technological knowledge on sustainability of resource management; and
  – evolve and introduce the appropriate technology by adopting and adapting indigenous technology to make them self reliant.

* More intensive research works may be undertaken to investigate the strengths and weaknesses of the forest policies and evolve certain workable models for effective community involvement in the sustainable forest management.

Bibliography

Ackerman F (1994). The natural interest rate of the forest : Macroeconomic requirements for sustainable development. *Ecological Economics, 10 (1)* : 21 - 26.

Adams W M (1990). *Green Development : Environment and Sustainability in the Third World.* Routledge Natural Environment Problems and Management Series, London & New York.

Adhikari J (1990). Is community forestry a new concept? An analysis of the past and present policies affecting forest management in Nepal. *Soc Nat Resour, 3 (3)* : 257 - 265.

Agrawal A (1996). The community vs the market and the state- Forest use in Indian Himalayas. *Journal of Agricultural & Environmental Ethics, 9 (1)* : 1 - 15.

Agrawal A and Narain S (1989). Towards Green Villages. A common strategy for environmentally sound and participatory rural development. Centre for Science and Environment, New Delhi.

Ahlback A J (1995). Mobilizing Rural People in Tanzania to Tree Planting: Why and How. *Ambio, 24(5):* 304 - 310.

Ahmad A (1995). Community based conservation efforts in Pakistan. In : *Nature Conservation 4 : The Role of Networks,* Eds Saunders D A, Craig J L & Mattiske E M, Surrey Beatty & Sons. pp 474 - 477.

Ahmad S (1994). Public participation and rural development in south Chhindwada forest (Madhya Pradesh). Indian Forester, *120 (7)* : 611-614.

Aird P L (1994). Conservation for the sustainable development of forests worldwide: concepts and terms. *Forestry Chronicle, 70 (6)* : 666 - 674.

Alam Sahabat (1987). Forest Resources Crisis in the Third World. Proc Conference on *Forest Resources Crisis in the Third World,* 6 - 8 Sept 1986, Malaysia.

Alam Sahabat (1988). *Global Development and Environment Crisis –Has Humankind a Future?* Asia Pacific People's Environment. Network, Malaysia.

Allen Robert (1980). *How to Save World : Strategy for World Conservation.* I U C N - U N E P - W W F. Mc Corquodale (Newton) Ltd.

Allender E B (1988). *Fuelwood Production Potential on Degraded and Under-utilised Sites.* Land and Energy Private Ltd. Senerac Project, South Australia.

Ameyaw S (1992). Sustainable development and the community: lessons from the KASHA project, Botswana. *Environmentalist, 12 (4) :* 267-275.

Andersen K E (1995). Institutional flaws of collective forest management. *Ambio, 24 (6) :* 349 - 353.

Anderson J, Clement J & Crowder I V, (1998). Accommodating conflicting interests in forestry concepts emerging from pluralism Unasylva, 49(3):3-10.

Anonymous (1995). Sustainable development – challenge for Asian growth. *International-Bulk-Journal, 15 (9) :* 77-79.

Arnold E M Jr (1991). *Community Forestry : Ten Years in Review.* Community Forestry Note 7. FAO, Rome.

Arnold J E M (1998). Managing factors as common property, Forestry Paper 136, FAO, Rome.

Arnold J E M and Stewart W C (1991). Common property resource management In India, Tropical Forestry Papers 24, Oxford Forestry Institute, University of Oxford, England.

Arnstein S R (1977). A ladder of citizen participation. In : *Eco-social Systems and Ecopolitics,* Ed Deutsch K W, UNESCO, Switzerland. pp 277 - 286.

Ashe Jeffrey (1979). *Assessing Rural Needs.* ACCION, AITEC, VITA. Cambridge.

Ascher William (1995). Communities and Sustainable Forestry in Developing Countries. International Centerfor Self-Governance. Institute of Contemporary Studies, San Francisco.

Asian Productivity Organisation (1989). *Forestry Resources Management.* Report of APO Symposium on Forestry Resources Management, Tokyo, Japan, 7-14 November.

Australian Government Publication Service (1976). *Ecological Effects of Increasing Human Activities on Tropical and Subtropical Forest Ecosystems.* Report on Symposium, University of Papua New Guinea Publication No 3, Canberra.

Australian Government Publication Service (1990). *Ecologically Sustainable Development.* A commonwealth discussion paper, Canberra.

Bahuguna V K Luthra V & Rathore B M S (1994). Collective Forest Management in India. *Ambio, 23(4-5):* 269-273.

Bahuguna V K (1992). Collective Resource Management, An experience in Harda Forest Division, Regional Centre for Wasteland Development, IIFM, Bhopal.

Bahuguna V K (1993). Forestry in Ecodevelopment, An experience in Jhabua Forest Division, Regional Centre for National Afforestation & Eco-development Board, IIFM, Bhopal.

Baland J M & Platteau J P (1996). Halting Degradation of Natural Resources: Is there a Role for Rural Communities, Clarendon Press, Oxford.

Barron D E & Rotherham T (1991). Towards sustainable development in industrial forestry. *Forestry Chronicle, 67 (2)*: 113-116.

Basiago A D (1994). Sustainable development in tropical forest ecosystems. *International Journal of Sustainable Development and World Ecology, 1 (1) :* 34-40.

Berkes F (1989). *Common Property Resources : Ecology and Community-based Sustainable Development.* Belhaven and I U C N.

Bhattacharya A K (1996). Sustainable forest management and community participation - in global perspective. Dissertation submitted as a part fulfilment of course on Environmental Management and Sustainable Forestry Development, in University of Tasmania, Australia.

Blackburn S (1993). *Practical Vsionaries - A Study of Community Aid Abroad.* Melbourne University Press. Australia.

Bliss J C (1996). The four Ps of forest management. *Journal of Forestry, 94 (4)* : 44.

Bromley D W and Cernea M M (1989). The Management of Common Property Natural Resources: Some conceptual and Operational fallacies. World Bank Discussion Paper No. 57. Washington DC, World Bank.

Bundyard P (1989). Guardians of the Forest : Indigenist Policies in the Colombian Amazon. *The Ecologist, 19(6):* 255-258.

Byron M & M Arnold (1999). What futures for the people of the tropical forests? World Development 27 (5).

Carter N & Brine J (1995). M F P Australia : a vision of sustainable development for a post-industrial society. *Planning Practice and Research, 10 (1)* : 25-43.

Chan C L W (1991). Grassroots participation in environmental protection-tactics of mobilization. In : Proc Asia and Pacific RegionalConference *'Environmental Protection and Social Development : Role of Non Governmental Organisations'*, August 26 - 31, Hongkong. pp. 169 - 176.

Chaplin Mac (1989). Ecodevelopment and wishful thinking. *The Ecologist, 19(6):* 259-261.

Clarke J & Scher S J (Eds) (1991). Participatory technology development in agroforestry : methods from a pilot project in Zimbabwe. In : *Agroforestry Systems, 15 (2-3)* : 217-228, Proc Workshop 'Methods for participatory on–farm agroforestry research', Nairobi, 1990.

Commonwealth of Australia (1992). *National Forest Policy Statement :* A new focus for Australia's Forests, Commonwealth of Australia.

Commonwealth of Australia (1994). *Aboriginal and Trees Strait Islander Commission Information Kit on Native*. Commonwealth of Australia, Canberra.

D'Silva E & Appanah S (1993). Forestry management for sustainable development. *E D I Policy Seminar Report, World Bank, 32* : 46.

Dasmann R F (1985). Achieving the sustainable use of species and ecosystems. *Landscape Plann, 12 (3)* : 211-219.

De Mello S, Boothroyd P, Matthew N & Sparrow K (1994). Discovering common meaning: planning community development education with first nations. *Plan Canada*, January, pp. 14-21.

Dennis S (1988). Incorporating public opinion surveys in national forest land resource planning. *Soc Nat Resour, 1 (4):* 301-316.

Dhar S K (1994). Rehabilitation of degraded tropical forest watersheds with people's participation. *Ambio, 23 (3):* 218-221.

Dwivedi A P (1993). *Forestry in India.* Surya Publications, New Delhi, India.

Dove M R (1995). The theory of social forestry intervention: the state of the art of Asia, Agroforestry system, 30:315-340.

Dovers S R & Handmer J W (1993). Contradictions in sustainability. *Environmental Conservation, 20 (3) :* 217-222.

E P A (1974). *Carrying Capacity in Regional Environmental Management.* Socioeconomic Environmental Studies Series. Office of Research and Development, U S Environmental Protection Agency, Washington, D C.

Editor (1990). Whose Common Future? *Ecologist, 20 (3):* 82-84.

Egger P & Majeres J (1992). Local resource management and development : strategic dimensions of people's participation. In : *Grassroots Environmental Action,* Eds Ghai D & Vivian J M, Routledge. pp 304-324.

Ehrlich P (1972). *The Population Bomb.* Pan / Ballantine, London, England.

Endress L H & Roumasset J A (1994). Golden rules for sustainable resource management. *Economic Record, 70 (210):* 266-277.

Falconer J (1990). The Major Significance of "Minor" Forest Products :The Local use and the Value of Forests in the West African Humid Forest Zone. Community Forestry Note 6, FAO, Rome.

F A O, U N (1985). *Tropical Forestry Action Plan.* Rome. Italy.

FAO (1991). *Plan of Action for People's Participation in Rural Development.* C 91/92. 26th session, 9-28 November, Rome.

FAO (1996). *Participation in Practice – lessons from People's*

Participation Programme.Rome. Italy.

FAO, UN (1986). *Forestry Extension Organisations.* SIDA, Rome, Italy.

Fellizer J F P (1994) : Achieving sustainable development through community-based resource management. *Regional Development Dialogue, 15 (1)* : 210-219.

Ferguson I S (1996). *Sustainable Forest Management.* Oxford University Press, Oxford, New York.

Fordham G (1995). Sustaining local involvement. *Community Development Journal, 28 (4)* : 299-304.

Gadgil M (1992). Conserving Biodiversity as if People Matter : A case study from India. *Ambio, 21(3):* 266-270.

Gadgil M, Berkes F & Folke C (1993). Indigenous knowledge of biodiversity conservation. *Ambio, 22 (2-3)* : 151-156.

Gadgil M & Guha R (1992). This Fissured land. Oxford University Press, New Delhi.

Gericke K L & Sullivan J (1994). Public participation and appeals ofForest Service plans – an empirical examination. *Soc Nat Resour, 7(2)* : 125-135.

Gibbs (1996). *The Aboriginies.* IV Ed. Longman.

Gibson R (1995). Better for nature, better for us : economic change for people and the environment. *Alternatives, 21 (4)* : 1-40.

Gilmour D A (1990). Resource availability and indigenous forest management systems in Nepal. *Soc Nat Resour, 3 (2):* 145-158.

Gilmour, D A & Fisher R J (1991). Villagers, Forests & Foresters: The Philosophy, Process and Practice of Community Forests in Nepal, Sahayogi Press, Kathmandu.

Glasby G P (1995). Concept of sustainable development : a meaningful goal? *Science of the Total Environment, 159 (1):* 67-80.

Godoy R. & Bawa K S (1993). The Economic value and sustainable harvest of plants and animals from the tropical forests: assumptions, hypotheses and methods. Economic Botany, 47: 215-219.

Grub M, Koch M, Thomson A and Sullivan (1995). *The Earth Summit Agreements : A Guide and Assessment.* An Analysis of the Rio'92 UN Conference on Environment and Development. Energy and Environment Programme, The Royal Institute of International Affairs, London, Earthscan Publications Ltd, London.

Grun Aniela (1996). *Community Management of Marine Protected Areas in Indonesia.* Draft Literature Review for BSc Honours, Centre for Environmental Studies, University of Tasmania, Hobart, Australia.

Gupta A (1988). *Ecology and Development in Third World.* Routledge, New York, U S A. pp. 80.

Henderson H (1994). Paths to sustainable development : the role ofsocial indicators. *Futures, 26 (2) :* 125-137.

Hewitt A W (1996). *The Native Tribes of South East Australia.* Aboriginal Students Press, Canberra.

Hill I and D. Sheilds (1998). Incentives for Joint Forest Management in India: Analytical Methods and Case studies. World Bank Technical papers No. 394, World Bank, Washington

Hinrichs N (1970). *Population, Environment and People.* Council on Population and Environment. Chicago, Illinois.

Ho W (1992). The process of participatory rural extension. *Network Paper: Rural Development Forestry Network, 14d :* 1-12.

Hobley M (1996). Participatory Forestry: The process of change in India and Nepal. Rural Development Forestry Study Guide, Overseas Development Institute.

Hummel F C (Ed) (1984). *Forest Policy : A Contribution to Resource Development.* Martinus Nijhoff / Dr W Junk Publishers, The Hague, Boston, Lancaster.

I U C N (1980). *World Conservation Strategy.* I U C N, Gland. Switzerland.

Jeffrey *et al.* (1998). Joint Forest Management : A silent revolution amongst forest department staff? Paper presented at the workshop on participatory Natural Resource Management 6th 7th April 1998, Mansfield College Oxford .

Jewitt S (1995). Voluntary and official forest protection committees in Bihar-solutions to India's deforestation. *Journal of Biogeography, 22 (6) :* 1003-1021.

Jodha N S (1990). Rural Common Property resources: Contribution & Crisis, Economic and Political Weekly. Quaterly review of agriculture, 25(26).

Johnson Kirk (1993). Reconciling rural communities and resource conservation. *Environment, 35* : 16-20.

Johnson S P (1993). *The Earth Summit : The United Nations Conference on Environment and Development.* International Environmental Law and Policy Series, Graham & Trotman / Martinus Nijhoff, London / Dordrecht / Boston.

Johnston B E (1993). Forests and U N C E D minutes 92 : a foundation for the future. *Forestry Chronicle, 69 (5) :* 539-544.

Josephson Julian (1992). Sustainable Forest Management. *Environmental Science and Technology, 26* : 1892-1894.

Kangas J (1994). An approach to public participation in strategic forest management planning. *For Ecol Manage, 70 (1-3):* 75-78.

Kasoma P M B, Ipulet P & Katabarwa D (1995). Local community participation in conservation : three case studies from Uganda. In : *Nature Conservation 4 : The Role of Networks*, Eds Saunders D A, Craig J L & Mattiske M, Surrey Beatty & Sons. pp 542-547.

Kessler W B, Salwasser H, Cartwright C W Jr & Caplan JA (1992). New perspectives of sustainable natural resources management. *Ecol Appl, 2 (3) :* 221-225.

Koenig K M & Headley Jean (1995). Sustainable forest management : where do you fit in? *Wood and Wood Products, 100 :* 43-47.

Kruger F J, Everard D A & Manders P T (1995). Forestry and environmentally sustainable development in South Africa. *Commonwealth Forestry Review, 74 (1) :* 71-75.

Larsen G L (1994). *Forest at UNCED : an emerging global consensus toward sustainability.* General Technical Report, US Department of Agriculture / Forest Service, PNW - GTR-336. pp 1-16.

Lay B (1996). *Community involvement in the establishment of an access network to scenic areas.* Paper presented at Best Tourism Practice Conference, Coolangatta, Australia.

Ludwig H F (1990). Moving toward Economic-cum-environmental sustainability in Asian developing countries. *The Environmentalist, 10 (4)* : 257-279.

Lynch, O J & Talbott K (1995). Balancing Acts: Community-Based Forest Management and National Law in Asia and the Pacific. World Resources Institute, Washington.

MPFD (1985). Madhya Pradesh Social Forestry Project, Second Mid term Evaluation, Madhya Pradesh Forest Department, Bhopal.

MPFD (1989). World Food programme-Assisted Project India 3227 "Rehabilitation of degraded forests and Afforestation in Madhya Pradesh", Madhya Pradesh Forest Department, Bhopal.

Mallik A U & Rahman H (1994). Community forestry in developed and developing countries: a comparative study. *Forestry Chronicle, 70 (6)* : 731-735.

Marcussen H S (1994). Improved natural resource management. The role of the state versus that of the local community. Occasional Paper, Roskilde University, *International Development Studies, 12* : 143-152.

Mathew K M (1986). Environmental awareness and ecodevelopment in India: a training programme for students. *Environ Conser, 13 (3)* : 351-353.

Mishra G (1994). The Budhikhamani model of Participatory Management of the Forest ecosystem in Orissa 120(7) 597-601.

Mgeni A S M (1992). Farm and Community Forestry (Village Afforestation) Programme in Tanzania : Can it go beyond Lipservice! *Ambio, 21(6):* 426-430.

Moffatt I (1994). On measuring sustainable development indicators. *International Journal of Sustainable Development and World. Ecology, 1 (2)* : 97-109.

Morris B (1986). Deforestation in India and the Fate of Forest Tribes. *The Ecologist, 16 (6)* : 253-257.

Morrison E & Bass S M J (1992). What about the people? In : *Plantation Politics,* Eds Sargent C & Bass S, Earthscan. pp 92-120.

Mortiss P (1993). *Extension for Rural Change*. II Ed. Department of Primary Industries, Queensland.

Mukherjee N (1995). Forest management and survival needs– community experience in West Bengal. *Economic and Political Weekly*, Bombay, *30 (49) :* 3130-3132.

Muntemba S (1989). Research for sustainable development : The role of NGOs. *Development, 2-3 :* 65-67.

Murrey C H (1991). Caring for forests in the changing world. *Forest Policy, 6 (3) :* 213-218.

Myers Norman (1995). Population and Biodiversity. *Ambio, 24 (1) :* 56-57.

Nagpal Tanvi (1995). Voices from the developing world: Progress towards sustainable development. *Environment, 37 :* 10-15.

National Wastelands Development Board (1991). *Guidelines for Microplanning*. NWDB, Ministry of Environment & Forests, Government of India, New Delhi.

Niuatui Petely (1991). *Sustainable Development for Tuvalu : A Reality or an Illusion!* Thesis, Centre for Environmental Studies, University of Tasmania, Hobart, Australia.

Oakley P (1991). The concept of participation in development. *Landscape Urban Ecol, 20 (1-3):* 115-122.

Orians G H (1990). Ecological concepts of sustainability. *Environment, 32 (9) :* 10-15.

Palit S (1972). Protection of Foreset in Purulia District, West Bengal Forests 2 (2, 3).

Park C C (1986). *Environmental Policies : An International Review*. Croom Helm. London.

Patnaik B.K. & Dutta S (1997). JFM in South West Bengal : A study in Participatory development. Economic and Political Weekly, Dec. 13, 1997.

Pearce D W & Warford J J (1993). *World without End: Economics, Environment, and Sustainable Development*. World Bank, Oxford University.

Poffenberger Mark (1995). India's Forest Keepers, Lovraj Kumar Memorial Lecture. SPWD/New Delhi.

Poffenberger M & Singh C (1996). In Poffenberger, M and B. McGean (ed), (1996), Village Voices, Forest Choices: Joint

Forest Management in India, Oxford University Press, Delhi.

Porter C F (1985). *Environment Impact Assessment: A Practical Guide.* University of Queensland Press, New York, London, St Lucia.

Postel S & Ryan J C (1991). Toward sustainable forestry worldwide. *Journal of Soil and Water Conservation, 46 (2):* 119-122.

Prance G T (1995). Systemics, Conservation and sustainable development. *Biodiversity and Conservation, 4 (5) :* 490-500.

Ramakrishnan P S (1992). Tropical forests. Exploitation, conservation and management. *Impact of Science on Society, 166 :* 149-162.

Rannard C D (1991). Sustainable development (in forestry) – what does it really mean? *Forestry Chronicle, 67 (2) :* 109-112.

Rao K & Geisler C (1990). The social consequences of protected areas development for resident populations. *Soc Nat Resour, 3 (1) :* 19-32.

Rastogi A (1995). Impact of Culture on Process of Joint Forest Management in India. *Ambio, 24(4):* 253-255.

Redcliff M (1992). Sustainable development and popular participation : a framework for analysis. In : *Grassroots environmental action,* Eds Ghai D & Vivian J M, Routledge. pp 23-49.

Redclift M (1992). The Meaning of Sustainable Development. *Geoforum, 23 (3) :* 395-403.

Redelsheimer C L (1996). Enhancing management through public involvement – an industrial landowners experience. *Journal of Forestry, 94 (5) :* 24-27.

Reid W V C (1989). Sustainable development: lessons from success. *Environment, 31 (4) :* 29-35.

Ribot J C (1995). From exclusion to participation : turning Senegal's forestry policy around? *World Development, 23 :* 1587-1599.

Robertson J (1990). *Future Wealth. A New Economics for 21st Century.* Cassels Publishers Ltd, England.

Rowan R J, Ross A & Walton W (1995). Sustainable development and the development control process. *Town Planning Review, 66 (3)* : 269-286.

Ryn Lyndall (1996). *The Aboriginal Tasmanians.* II Ed. Allen & Unwin, NSW, Australia.

Sadler B (1990). Sustainable development, northern realities and the design and implementation of the regional conservation strategies. In : '*Achieving Sustainable development through Northern Conservation Strategies'*, University of Calgary Press, Calgary. pp 3-31.

Sarin M (1993). From conflict to collaboration: local institutions in joint forest management. Joint Forest Management Working Paper No. 14, SPWD and Ford Foundation, New Delhi.

Saunders A D, Craig J L & Mattiske E M (1996). *The Role of Networks : Nature Conversation.* Four volumes. Surrey Beatty & Sons Pty Ltd.

Saxena N C (1992). Farm Forestry and Land use in India : Some Policy Issues. *Ambio, 21 (6)* : 420-425.

Saxena N C (1997). The Saga of Participatory Forest Management In India. CIFOR Special Publication, CIFOR.

Schumacher E F (1973). *Small is beautiful : Economics as if the people mattered.* Harper & RO Publishers Inc, NY, USA.

Schwartz T (1989). The Brazilian Forest People's Movement. The *Ecologist, 19 (6):* 245-247.

Sharma R A (1995). Participatory Forest Management in India. *Ambio, 24 (2)* : 131-133.

Shea S (1993). Sustainable management of the forests for multiple use benefits: Is there anything new under the sun? *Commonwealth Forestry Review, 72 (4)* : 242 - 255.

Smith P (1996). Aboriginal participation in forest management - not just another stakeholder. *Forestry Chronicle, 72 (1)* : 2.

SPWD (1993). Joint Forest Management Update-1993 Society for promotion of wastelands Development, New Delhi.

SPWD (1998). Joint Forest Management Update-1993 Society for Promotion of Wastelands Development, New Delhi.

Sonnteg N C, Everitt R R, Rattie L C, Colnett D L, Wolf C P,

Truett J C, Dorcey A H J & Holling C S (1989). *Cumulative Effects Assessment : A Context for Research and Development*. Canadian Environmental Assessment Research Council. Ministry of Supply & Services,Canada.

Srisarin R (1994). *Public Participation in Forest Management in Thailand.* Thesis. Centre for Environmental Studies, Department of Geography & Environmental Studies. University of Tasmania, Australia.

Starke L (1990). *Signs of Hope : Working towards our Common Future.* Oxford Univ Press. Great Britain.

Starke Linda Ed (1995). Pakistan Nation Conservation Strategy. IUCN–The World Conservation Union, Pakistan.

Stewart F (1977). *Technology and Underdevelopment.* McMillan, England.

Stocker L J (1995). Community Science and community scientists: their roles in conservation. In : *Nature Conservation 4 : The Role of Networks,* Eds Saunders D A, Craig J I & Mattiske E M, Surrey Beatty & Sons. pp 548-554.

Tasmanian Public Land Use Commission (1996). *Inquiry into areas to be reserved under the Tasmanian-Commonwealth Regional Forest Agreement.* Background Report Part A, Tasmanian Public Land Use Commission.

The Economist (1986). *Giving India's Trees to the People.* Feature Article, *301* : 101-102.

The Indian Forester (2000). *Joint Forest Management : Retrospect and New Intitatives.* Vol 125 (5), May 2000.

Thin N, Neeraj P & Prafulla Gorada, (1998). Muddles about the Middle: NGOs as Intermediaries in JFM. Edinburgh Papers in South Asian Studies Number 12, Department of Social Anthrolpology, University of Edinburgh, Edinburgh.

Tinker I (1994). Women and community forestry in Nepal : Expectations and realities. *Soc Nat Resour, 7 (4)* : 467-481.

Trainer T (1990). Rethinking sustainable development. *Geog Educ 6 (2)* : 24.

Townson, I.M. (1995). Forest Products and Household Income: A Review and Annotated Bibliography.

Tropical Forestry Papers 31. Centre for International Forestry

Research and Oxford Forestry Institute, Oxford.

United Nations (1990). *State of the Environment in Asia and the Pacific.* Economic and Social Commission for Asia and the Pacific. Bangkok, Thailand.

Vivian J M (1991). Greening at the grassroots : people's participation in sustainable development. *Discussion Paper, United Nations Research Institute for Social Development. 22 :* 25.

Wells M & Brandon K (1995). *Linking Protected Area Management with Local Communities.* The World Bank, WWF and US Agency for International Development, Washington, D C.

Wells M P (1995). Community based forestry and biodiversity projects have promised more than they have delivered. Why is this and what can be done? In : *Management of Tropical Forests,* University of Oslo, Centre for Development & the Environment, *1 (95) :* 269-286.

White W A (1991). Economics and sustainable forest development: the case of soil degradation. *Forestry Chronicle, 67 (1) :* 19-22.

Wiersum K F (1995). 200 years of sustainability in forestry : lessons from history. *Environ Manage, 19 (3) :* 321-329.

Wight P A (1993). Sustainable ecotourism : balancing economic, environmental and social goals within an ethical framework. *Jour Tourism Studies, 4(2):* 54-66.

World Bank (1990). *Indonesia : Sustainable Development of Forests, Landand Water.* A World Bank Country Study, Washington, DC.

World Bank (1994). *Indonesia : Environment and Development.* A World Bank Country Study, the World Bank, Washington, DC.

World Bank (1995). India : Madhya Pradesh Forestry Project. *Appraisal Report No. 12408-IN.*

World Commission on Environment and Development (1987). *Our Common Future.* Oxford University Press, Oxford, New York.

World Resources Institute, IUCN UNEP (1992). *Global Biodiversity Strategy.* IUCN, Gland, Switzerland.

INDEX